The Scholarship & Financial Aid Solution

How to Go to College for Next to
Nothing with Short Cuts, Tricks and Tips
from Start to Finish Revised

2nd Edition

DEBRA LIPPHARDT

The Scholarship & Financial Aid Solution: How to Go to College for Next to Nothing with Short Cuts, Tricks and Tips from Start to Finish Revised 2nd Edition

Copyright © 2015 by Atlantic Publishing Group, Inc.

1405 SW 6th Ave. • Ocala, Florida 34471 • **352-622-1825** • 352-622-1875–Fax

Web site: www.atlantic-pub.com • E-mail: sales@atlantic-pub.com

SAN Number: 268-1250

Library of Congress Cataloging-in-Publication Data

Lipphardt, Debra, 1954-
   The scholarship & financial aid solution: how to go to college for next to nothing with short cuts, tricks and tips from start to finish / by Debra Lipphardt. -- Revised Second edition.
      pages cm
   Includes bibliographical references and index.
   ISBN 978-1-60138-950-3 (alk. paper) -- ISBN 1-60138-950-7 (alk. paper) 1. Scholar-ships--United States--Handbooks, manuals, etc. 2. Student aid--United States--Handbooks, manuals, etc. I. Title. II. Title: Scholarship and financial aid solution.
   LB2338.L57 2015
   378.3'4--dc23
                           2014035878

Printed in the United States
BOOK PRODUCTION DESIGN: T.L. Price • design@tlpricefreelance.com

Over the years, we have adopted a number of dogs from rescues and shelters. First there was Bear and after he passed, Ginger and Scout. Now, we have Kira, another rescue. They have brought immense joy and love not just into our lives, but into the lives of all who met them.

We want you to know a portion of the profits of this book will be donated in Bear, Ginger and Scout's memory to local animal shelters, parks, conservation organizations, and other individuals and nonprofit organizations in need of assistance.

– Douglas & Sherri Brown,
President & Vice-President of Atlantic Publishing

Author Biography

Debra Lipphardt is happily married with two grown children, Jessica and Michael. She can now add the wonderful title of 'Nonnie', (aka grandma) to a special little girl, Aubrey, who brings a bright ray of sunshine into all of their lives. Making up and telling stories to Aubrey, as she did previously to her own children, has brought back Debra's desires and dreams to once again, return to her vision of writing her book of fairy tales.

Debra is the Career and College Center Specialist and Scholarship Coordinator for a public high school in Florida. Scholarships instantly became her passion upon meeting and being inspired by so many wonderful young people needing assistance to pay for college. After being asked many times to tell how her students have been so accomplished at obtaining scholarships, she decided to share her knowledge by writing it down and putting it into a book, hoping to help others outside of her community

<u>*Author Dedication*</u>

I want to dedicate the second edition of my book first of all to my wonderful family. They have always encouraged and supported me in everything, from my writing to any other dreams I have reached towards. And of course to the special addition to our family, my granddaughter Aubrey. Her laughter, personality, and love, keeps me going, warms my heart, and makes me want to be a better person.

Next I would like to recognize my very good friends, who are always there for me through the good times and bad.

Also to the students that inspired me to write a book on scholarships. I dedicate this to the hundreds upon hundreds of students who have passed through my life, making such an impact on me and enriching my life.

And lastly, thank you dad for teaching me to be the best I can be and to never give up and to dream the impossible dream!

Table of Contents

Introduction

I have always enjoyed writing short stories and have entertained the thought of writing a novel in the future, but my idea of writing always leaned toward fairy tales filled with suspense. So what turned out to be my first book? A non-fiction book about scholarships; such a shock to me! I remember reading that a first-time writer should write about something he or she is familiar with or something he or she enjoys. Well, I love working with scholarships, have done extensive research, and have given countless lectures and workshops on them. So when I 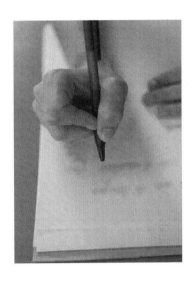 decided to finally begin my 'great American novel', I sat down and started this book. So much for fairy tales, but this still turned out to be happily ever after.

I am writing this book not only for the students, but also as a guide for parents and other school personnel to assist them in aiding students with scholarships. This comes from me as a mom of a daughter now teaching elementary school, a son who is a firefighter, and also as a College and Career Center Specialist/Scholarship Coordinator.

I was first introduced to the world of scholarships when I began working in the guidance office at a local high school. A few scholarship applications and advertisements came in the mail and intrigued my interest. No one had ever even mentioned the word scholarships to me when I was in high school, so questions erupted in my head. How much could students actually benefit from these scholarships? Were they easy to obtain? Where could you find them? How could students apply? How can a student win?

There were a variety of requirements, and each application differed from the other. I investigated different scholarships and applications that came in and looked elsewhere to find more. To my surprise, there were many more than I could ever imagine. My position changed from the guidance office to College and Career Center Specialist, and I added 'Scholarship Coordinator' to my title, which allowed me to work with students even more. I created this position on my own because my actual job did not include working with scholarships to the extent that I do. I do most of the work on my own time at home – because I love doing it.

After finding so many diverse scholarships, I started looking for eligible students, matching them up with each type of scholarship and encouraging them to apply. I persuaded, begged, or nagged-whatever it took, students to submit applications. When they actually started receiving money from scholarships, I became excited. From then on, I hunted down more and more scholarships.

I discovered scholarship opportunities everywhere. I found them in stores, heard about them on the radio, and read about them in the newspaper and public library. I searched free websites under different names, genders, races, and college majors and found many websites that charge fees in order to apply, but this can be avoided and will be further explained in Chapter 11.

As a Scholarship Coordinator, I hold an annual scholarship workshop for students and parents. I have lectured at local clubs, churches, parent workshops, and organizations and have been interviewed by several local radio stations (and even a few out-of-state). I have received various awards, including two countywide "School Employee of the Year" awards, local club awards, and several Veterans of Foreign Wars (VFW) awards through my work. I'm merely stating my honors to verify and showcase my experiences and credentials on this topic.

I've worked with students who applied for scholarships for the past 15 years. Our high school, one of six in the county, has won the most awards almost each year. In fact, my school's seniors have done so well over the last fourteen years that they've won at least twice the amount than any of the other six county high schools at the County Awards Night. Our seniors have averaged over five million dollars' worth of scholarships. This amount consists of all the different scholarships, including athletics, college-awarded scholarships and the Florida Bright Futures as well.

I feel overjoyed whenever one of my students tells me he or she received a scholarship. I've had numerous students from the past thank me for my assistance when I helped them make it possible to pay for college. Their gratitude makes the all the toilsome hours spent at home worth the while.

I was able to help my own children receive scholarships as well. When I discovered the wonderful world of scholarships, they were only in elementary and middle school. At that time, I didn't think about how this would affect them. I never thought that all my work would pay off personally when they applied for scholarships.

My daughter won enough money to cover her tuition and books for the first two years, and even had money left over for the last two years of college. My son, four years later, was also able to put leftover money in the bank after his first two years of college as well. Yes, I had to push them, just like most seniors, to apply for any scholarship they were eligible for—but it paid off. They were both in the top 20 percent of their class, had average ACT scores, served more than 100 hours of community service, and were involved in sports and other clubs. They competed against students who had even higher grades, test scores, and many more community service hours than they did, yet my son and my daughter still won, sometimes just because of how they answered their essay questions.

I cannot guarantee that everyone will win a scholarship, but I have found that everyone has a chance. The odds are higher, of course, if you have excellent grades, participate in many extracurricular activities, and rack up volunteer hours; you'll merely be more eligible for a larger number of scholarships, it's as simple as that.

One of my most memorable experiences involved a young student with a less than average GPA (grade point average). He came from an impoverished background and lived in a very disadvantaged neighborhood. This young man had a great personality, and we talked often about his outlook on life and dreams for the future. There was just one problem: financial support. There was a women's club that dispersed scholarships every year but were for females only. I worked with the head of the scholarship committee and convinced her to give the scholarship to a male student that year. She asked if I had any suggestions, and I told her about a great young man I knew and giving him a scholarship would impact his world. Not only did the committee award him $2,000 but the scholarship was also renewed the following year (and each year after that until he graduated). I ran into him two years later and learned that he was working his way through college with the help of his scholarships. I introduced him to my mother and sister, and he sat down and started talking to them. He told them that without the scholarships he would have never left his neighborhood; that money made all the difference and bettered his life. He made me feel like I made a difference in his life. That feeling was one of the most rewarding experiences in my life. His enthusiasm and genuine gratitude only increased my desire to help more students win scholarships and achieve their dreams.

That's where this book comes in. I hope that it will assist and inspire you to apply for scholarships in the present or future.

Chapter 1:
SCHOLARSHIPS 101

The majority of scholarships that students are eligible for are open during their senior year in high school. Many adults expect students to take on all the responsibility and do it themselves. Even the most mature seniors still manage to catch that invisible, contagious disease called "senioritis." Unfortunately, many realize, when it is too late, that they have a very limited financial assistance in college, besides the loans. Transitioning from high school to college is a very confusing time in their lives. They are on the road to maturity but still don't  understand everything; they are only beginning the journey to adulthood. Seniors still need some guidance and encouragement from parents and other mentors. You can help them win scholarships by reminding them to continuously search for eligibility, turn the applications in on time and check their status. You can also help them by brainstorming and proofreading for grammatical errors. Your support will help them go farther than they could on their own. Parents and teachers, need to remember that they are still children and need direction. You would not believe the number of students who still contact me after graduation, seeking ways to pay for college. All I can do is advise them to go their college's financial aid office, 'Google' foundation scholarships (scholarships from private sources for that particular college), and to go on many different scholarship search websites.

Most seniors and their parents don't realize how much college costs. I've had many students tell me that college won't cost them anything, either through Florida Bright Futures scholarships (which is a Florida program for students who attend a Florida college or university) or through the International Baccalaureate Program. In the past, Florida Bright Futures used to pay for 75 to 100 percent of students' tuition if they attended a public college in Florida, but now it only pays between $48 and $103 per credit hour, which comes out to about 40 percent of tuition costs. Students have to meet certain strict criteria, such as a high GPA, taking specific classes, and high ACT or SAT scores; only then would they qualify. Unfortunately, the most commonly obtained Bright Futures scholarship, the Florida Medallion, increased its SAT/ACT criteria by such a high margin that it's almost impossible for even the average student to receive the award. The International Baccalaureate (IB) students in Florida can earn the Bright Futures Florida Academic Scholarship with their diploma, but this doesn't even cover half the costs any longer. Students should check with their guidance counselors to see if their state has something similar (see Chapter 10).

These programs only cover partial tuition for up to four years, and in the case of IB students (if they have their diploma and start as a second-year college student), only 15 hours past a bachelor's degree, but it only covers the bachelor degree's tuition. If students plan on receiving their master's or other graduate degrees, that tuition is no longer covered. These scholarships don't offer full rides; they only cover a fraction of expenses. The most expensive cost is room and board, unless you attend a private institution. When you have to pay for room and board, books, and other fees, this is where it really adds up.

The cost of college education, like everything else, keeps escalating. Unfortunately, tuition for a public university or college is only a small portion of total costs. Room and board can sometimes triple the amount of tuition. As of now, in Florida, a public college's tuition (if you're a state resident) averages around $6,000 per year, books cost about $1,000 per year, and room and board are about $8,000 or more per year.

College is expensive, but you don't have to pay the full amount if you do it right. There are local, state, and national scholarships, as well as state and federal grants. Students can also borrow federal loans with low-interest rates, but loans should be used as a last resort. Free money is the best way to go.

There are so many different types of scholarships that are possible to obtain with research and determination. The practical, common sense method to winning scholarships is "apply and apply, again and again." Do not give up. It isn't guaranteed that everyone will win a scholarship, but you will definitely lose out if you don't even try. No student walks away from my classroom without at least two or three different applications in their hands, despite what his or her grades are or how extensive his or her outside school involvement is.

The following chapters will discuss scholarship requirements, where to find them, and how to fill out applications. I will also go over building up résumés and how you can use them with applications, tips on essays and letters of recommendations, and application shortcuts. Throughout this book, I will reiterate certain information in different ways and more in depth; I believe that the more you hear or read something, the more attention you pay to it. This book was written for students, as well as parents or other involved adults. But when it comes to the actual scholarship application, the student must do *all* the work, which includes following the directions, paying attention to deadlines, applying for the right scholarship, writing a knock-out essay and filling out the application.

CHAPTER 2:
TYPES OF SCHOLARSHIPS

There are so many different scholarships, each with specific requirements. The most common are based on a combination of academics, awards and honors received, SAT and/or ACT test scores, extracurricular activities, and community service. Other scholarships are based solely on community service or just for an essay written by the student. There are also scholarships based on the student's major or on financial need.

When an application has a specific requirement only, such as community service, academic achievements, leadership, or an extracurricular activity, you must have experience in whichever subject they are looking for. But most scholarships have general requirements. For example, you may have only a few hours of volunteer work because you are involved in sports or work. This is taken into consideration because your particular endeavor still shows student involvement. Work experience can also be substituted for other activities. On the other hand, you may have a plethora of community service hours or other extracurricular involvement and don't have time for a job. The main aspect that many scholarships look for is some type of involvement beyond schooling. Scholarship judges want to know that you are doing something besides going home to watch TV, play video games, or sleep.

Before going any further, I will explain and define the most common requirements in detail. Later in the book (Chapters 5 and 6), you will use this information to help you fill out applications.

Academics (Educational):

Academics include your overall grade point average (GPA) during high school. If a student's been dedicated all four years, then he or she will shine through. However, it usually takes a year or two for many students to realize how important grades are. This "growing up"  process can also be taken into consideration if students improve drastically during the last two or three years. They can write an explanation about why their work ethic or view on the importance of grades changed in some required essays. This falls under 'obstacles overcome' category.

There are, of course, more serious problems that students have to overcome, such as a learning disability, poverty, neglect or abuse, divorce, or a death in the family. These tribulations can definitely affect a student's grades. The student should take full advantage and let the scholarship committee know about these obstacles to showcase how he or she overcame adversity. This topic also shows that students were able to persevere and be successful in the end.

SAT and/or ACT scores also fall under academics. Most colleges accept scores from either test, but a select few prefer the SAT. These scores are on your transcripts, as long you filled in the required school code on the application. National-level scholarships may also request scores to be sent directly from the test site.

A very common requirement for most applications is an official transcript to validate your grades and test scores. You can usually get these from the guidance counselor's office. Transcripts include all your high school classes and semester/yearly grades, test scores, and sometimes various activities and service hours. Official transcripts come in a sealed envelope and must not be opened. If you do, the transcript will no longer be official. If the application does not require an official transcript, then there will usually be a place for your guidance counselor to sign and verify your grades and test scores. Because many scholarships are now online, you may have to upload your transcripts to complete the application. If you do not have a scanner, then ask someone at school (or a friend) who does. He or she can scan and send the transcript to your email, and you can upload it to the application.

Awards and Honors (Talents/Awards/Honors)

The awards and honors section varies. Some applications want you to list all awards or honors, while others ask specifically for academic awards and honors or non-academic awards and honors.

Academic awards include your program of study such as honors classes, Advanced Placement (AP) classes, the International Baccalaureate Program, ACE, or dual enrollment. These courses show that you've taken a rigorous curriculum path. You should also list classes that pertain to your major, such as assisting a teacher, for those going into education or health classes for those going into the medical field, because this shows that you are serious about your chosen career path.

Other academic recognitions include class rank or whether the student is graduating with honors, high honors, or highest honors (refer to Chapter 4, under 'Education'). You can list this as "will graduate with honors," or if you are unsure, you can list it as "plan to graduate with honors." Even if the student's grades are below a 3.0 but he or she has been on the honor roll a few times, the student can list "honor roll" as one of their academic awards. If you only took a few honors or AP classes, you can write that as "various honors and/or AP classes." There will be more detail on this in Chapters 4 and 5.

Another academic achievement is being a member of the National Honors Society. Even though it also counts as a membership in an organization, it still goes under 'awards' because the student was invited to be a member due to their academic (and in some schools, discipline, too) history. There is a math club called Mu Alpha Theta at the school I work. This class would be listed as an academic award because you must receive an invitation to become a member. If you were invited to be in one of these academic honors clubs and declined, you may still list it, but only as a nominee. Just remember that being a nominee is not as strong as being a member.

You should also include any other awards you have won as a result of your grades. Students need to keep track of every award they receive in high school including classroom awards (i.e. math, science, English) or any faculty-selected awards. The last two categories are not always considered as the best awards to receive, but they're still recognizing an achievement in the classroom. Some teacher took the time to honor that student. Any award is an outstanding accomplishment. A more prestigious award, though, would be if the student is the only one who receives the class award at the end of the year. This would mean that they have been chosen over any other student from that particular teacher's classes. They would list this achievement as "English Award - Student of the Year".

If a student is a member of an academic team, this would be considered an academic award, just as attending any summer college programs would go under this heading, too. Both of these entail academic achievements from the student.

Non-academic awards include being a captain of a team, an officer of a club, a member of a varsity team, and any other awards the student may have received from a sport, club, or organization. Another type of non-academic award is a volunteer (or community service) award, which is usually harder to come by, as you need a considerable amount of hours to receive this. If you've been selected to represent your school for a schol-arship or leadership position in the community, then these achievements would be considered a type of non-academic award, unless they were based on grades; then it would fall under the academic award category. Another benefit from being an officer, captain, or on the varsity team is leadership. Applicants stand out from the rest when they display strong leadership skills.

Leadership

Leadership skills aren't required for all scholarship applications, yet you will see this section on many of them. This is also a basic question on some college admissions applications. Students need to really think about their answer to this  section because leadership can be demonstrated in a variety of ways.

The city I live in has a leadership youth board that nominates students who undergo an interview to be selected for the board. They also must have a certain GPA and clean discipline record. This attained position would go under leadership positions or under the academic awards section if there is no leadership section.

Being an officer of a club, a captain on a team or a member of student council or government are obvious leadership positions, but there are other types as well. You might have led a committee, coached a younger team, tutored someone, taken care of younger children, or even directed your co-workers. These situations show that your leadership skills set an example for others. You could've helped organize a project in one of your classes or led a group who helped make a difference, even a small one. These acts of service display qualities of leadership. Think hard—you've probably applied some form of leadership skills to a situation without even realizing it.

Test Scores

Listing SAT and/or ACT scores is a common requirement on a majority of scholarship applications. In Florida, CPT or PERT tests can substitute for the SAT or ACT, but they are for community-college admissions only. Many students prefer to take these exams rather than the SAT or ACT, because they seem easier and are less expensive, but they've never been required on any scholarship application I've ever seen. I always urge students to start taking the SAT or ACT during the spring semester of their junior year, not only for college and Florida Bright Futures, but for scholarship applications as well.

These tests are expensive, and most students usually take them more than once. Students from low income-families can use waivers, usually twice per year during their junior and senior years, if they receive free or reduced lunches. They should visit their guidance counselor to see if they qualify.

You do not have to have the highest scores to win certain scholarships because many other factors are considered. Taking the exams shows that students are serious about going to college. However, if the scholarship is based solely on academics or if you are applying for any national academic type scholarships, the higher the scores are the better chances you will have to win.

The main difference between the tests is the sections. The SAT is divided into math and verbal, whereas the ACT is divided into math, reading, verbal, and science. Both tests include a written essay, which most four-year colleges require. I encourage my students to take both college prep tests because it's always a good idea to see which one you did better on; most students score higher on one than the other. If you need to retake it for higher scores, you can concentrate on the exam you did the best on. Students who test well on math tend to do better on the SAT. Some students, though, will score high on both tests. One trick to remember is answering all of the questions you know first then going back to finish the rest of them. However, on the ACT, you should take an educated guess on questions you cannota answer because you have a 20 percent chance of getting the questions right. Currently, you shouldn't do this on the SAT because an incorrect answer counts more against you than an unanswered one. There are a couple of different tricks to help you remember the difference between both tests: ACT stands for 'act' like you know it, or A is for 'answer everything'. However, the SAT will have major changes by spring 2016, such as no penalty for wrong answers, more applicable terminology and focusing on relevant math. Starting fall 2016, students should answer *all* of the questions on the SAT, as well as the ACT.

Extracurricular Activities

Extracurricular activities include recreation before or after school hours and not receiving grades, credit, or payment for participation. They can be school-related or non-school related as well. As long you meet at least once monthly and in an organized manner, you can  even count the Butterfly Club as an extracurricular activity. These activities show dedication, commitment, and involvement beyond the required school courses and hours. They also show that you'll grow up to be a productive, caring member of your community. Extracurricular activities include clubs (in your school or in your community), sports (inside or outside of school), being a member of your student government or a class representative, or participating in youth group or church choir. Students can even include lessons such as music, dancing, and acting, as well as any competitions, such as Motocross racing or gymnastics. Scholarship panels, as well as college admissions, like to see these types of commitments. It's much more impressive to join only one or two organizations for three or four years rather than join multiple ones for only a short period of time. The person who belongs to seven clubs for only a short time lacks commitment and appears to only join organizations to look good on paper.

Joining the school band or ROTC can also count as extracurricular activities, as long as students participate in them after or before school hours. If you get a grade or credit for the activity, just remember, it's no longer considered extracurricular. Many students belong to community concert bands or choirs outside of school, which counts as both extra-curricular and community service.

Remember to always list the number of years you belonged to any position or office you held (this also refers back to leadership). Include any type of awards you received as part of that club or sport, unless you listed that award somewhere else on the application. Repetition, or as students refer to it, "double dipping", isn't desirable, unless it stresses an important point or skill. This will be discussed again in Chapters 4 and 5.

There are usually service clubs or academic clubs in most schools that students can join. However, there are some clubs that are selective. Many clubs have a "cap," meaning there is only a certain number of students who can join or may have specific requirements for eligibility. You also can always start your own club, usually with a set of bylaws that include what it requires to be a member. Founding a club would also be an example of leadership skills and developing the club racks up service hours. Students need to see their activity director or principal to find out what they need to start a new organization.

I am actually a sponsor for a new club at the school where I work. There was a need for a club that allowed everyone to earn community service hours without exclusions. Five girls arranged simple bylaws for a club that included everybody. Students only needed to have least a 2.0 GPA (countywide criteria), attend one of two meetings a month, and commit to two hours of community service per month. There isn't a cap for receiving maximum community service hours either. The club, called the Pink

Ladies Service Club (from John Travolta's movie, *Grease*), was created with over 150 members. The Pink Ladies Service Club is now the largest and most active club at the school and is recognized by the community as a full-fledged service club. This club has taught them how to make a difference in their community, leadership skills, and gives out scholarships to senior members. Many have won several other scholarships because of their participation and community service in the club. Other students have started interest-related clubs at school, such as an environment club, a cancer aid club, Alzheimer's club, anime club, poetry club, or even a chemistry club. Take something that you're interested in, talk with friends, and go to your student activity director or the principal to get started.

Always remember that an extracurricular activity is any type of organization you belong to and that you actively participate in. You do not need to be the leader to be a large factor in your club because a club cannot function without members. Most organizations are also a good way to become involved in community service projects that involve helping others or making your community a better place to live in.

Community Service/Volunteering

Community service involves helping a non-profit organization or needy individuals for free. Helping your family does not count, nor can you receive pay for it. Also, community service given by a judge, (which is not voluntary), does not count toward community service hours either. Believe it or not, this question is asked every year.

There are numerous ways to receive service hours and many different places that need your help. You can pick and choose the one that is right for you. For example, if you feel that you want to go into the medical field, you should volunteer at a hospital or clinic. However, if you volunteer at a doctor's office, veterinarian's office, or dentist's office, (which are for-profit organizations) it cannot count towards community service hours. You can still include it but under the 'extracurricular' section. You should state that it was volunteer work under this section though because most scholarship committees will take the hours into consideration. Most importantly, your specified volunteer work shows that you are serious about your career path.

Church is also a great type of community service. You could be part of the choir, be an usher, help with technical work, or maybe teach Sunday school. Helping your church in any way counts for community service hours except, of course, attending church services. Include mission trips (local, out-of-state, or out of the country) as well.

Students often have more hours than they realize. One year, I approached a young man who was ranked fifth in his class and had extremely high test scores (he only missed one question on the SAT), but had never applied for a scholarship. I discussed his academics and college choices and asked him why he had never picked up any scholarship applications. He told me that he didn't belong to any clubs, had never participated in any sports, and didn't have any service hours, so he felt ineligible. When I asked him what he did during his spare time, he told me he helped out at his church and even had a sidewalk Sunday school that went to poorer parts of town every Sunday. I told him that his church involvement was a great source of community service. He thought that what he was doing was just his way of giving back to others and a natural part of his life, not community service. He started applying for scholarships, and when the county had its annual awards night, he won so many scholarships that people jokingly wanted to rename the awards ceremony after him.

There are so many great places to volunteer, and the rewarding experience is so much more than just service hours. Students have shared with me time and time again, the great feeling they get when they help others. Knowing that you can make a difference, even if it is only small, can empower you. I have met so many amazing students who accomplish fantastic things, and I love knowing that our future is in good hands. Volunteering is an excellent life-learning experience for all.

Whether you help a Girl Scout or Boy Scout troop, a sports team, the Explorers, Habitat for Humanity, the Humane Society, an environmental group, a local school, a museum, the Salvation Army, the American Cancer Society, or any other organization, including the community as a whole, there are so many avenues for you to explore. This is also a good time to experiment with your career choices. Many students have found a path to follow through their community service. If they find somewhere to volunteer that interests them, it will become a normal part of life for them. With our economy being down, anything a student does to help the needy or homeless is increasingly encouraged on a large amount of scholarship applications.

Community service activities seem to have trends just like everything else. More recently, bullying is a strong topic because of some of the terrible consequences. Therefore, anti-bully campaigns are needed and are also a good way to volunteer. Students who go to local elementary schools and mentor kids who are bullies or have been bullied are praised for their work and efforts. Most of them can relate to children and are able to help them find ways to prevent bullying. In fact one of my student's had over 800 hours in volunteering for the local soup kitchen, over 200 hours in church activities, and also helped start an Anti-Bully Campaign at our school. She only had 15-20 hours with this new endeavor as a mentor, but during an interview with a scholarship committee for a community-based scholarship (which she won), that was main topic they questioned her on. Mentoring is community service but goes much deeper than just adding up hours. It makes high school students rethink everything that they say and do. Volunteering is a two-way street. Usually, you can get more out of it than what you put in.

Students should include any hours that they spend in helping their clubs or any other organization. Whether it's setting up for meetings, cleaning up after events, or performing a play, every hour counts towards your total service hours. Another good example of volunteering is being an officer of a club. This includes preparing, planning, or leading meetings and events. You should also count hours such as making calls to set up activities and filling out any type of paperwork (insurance, permission forms, etc.) for an event.

When listing service hours on a scholarship application, make sure to list the hours and the number of years for each activity. If you are an officer, you can keep hours such as organizing and delegating, separate from the actual activity if you wish. But always keep track of the hours you spend as a leader because the number of hours adds up even for just one event. You can also list different projects you worked on separately and not under the club, especially if they required a plethora of hours.

You must always include the hours spent on community service, or scholarship panelists will think that it was only for a short amount of time. There are several ways to do this. You can put a total number of hours and years, or hours per year and number of years, or hours per week (or month) and number of years. If you put 'two hours weekly' and do not put the number of years, then they most likely will assume you just started that project. If you only list the number of years, without hours, then it looks like you just do it once or twice a year. Students need to take credit for all that they do. When listing the total hours on one event, it's a good idea to list the number of years as well because if you have hundreds of hours, such as 350, it's more realistic that the total amount was accomplished over two or three years, instead of one.

If your service hours vary, and have a few hours at one place and at another, then you need to combine them. If you put down just two or three hours several times, it looks inconsistent. Adding hours up (events that are less than 10) looks better than spacing them out. Write "various community service hours" with the total amount, and under that, list the events. If the volunteer hours are related (such as working with children but at different places) you can write for the activity, "assist various children-related events", the hours, and then what each activity was under it.

There are many scholarships that are interested only in community service hours. Typically, grades, extracurricular activities or financial status aren't required. This kind of scholarship is great for those with tons of service hours. Students usually are required to write an  essay on volunteering and how it's impacted him or her. Grades do not play a factor in most of these scholarships. However, there are some that take grades and extracurricular activities into consideration, too. When there are students who are equal (competition-wise) in community service hours, grades or other activities may influence the final decision.

Once again, it's extremely important to keep track of all of your hours in any type of community service. Usually, students turn in their hours (signed by someone you worked for) to the guidance counselor or the student activity director, and they record the hours in the computer, so that it's on the student's transcripts. Students should make sure they document all hours, dates and time, and descriptions with the correct amount of hours. Remember that you need to count everything, including planning time (such as putting together a project or even Sunday school plans for a class), time spent traveling to and from the volunteer destination (as long as it is local), and the actual hours you are helping. All of these hours count. Keep track of all hours and in which year you did community service. There are a few scholarships that want the hours of a certain time period or hours per each year in high school.

Another good idea is making a copy of everything you turn in because people make mistakes and misplace or lose paperwork all the time. If this happens, you won't need to worry—you'll be prepared.

Volunteering not only benefits those around you, but it also makes you a better person at the same time. Winning scholarships for helping others and bettering yourself is an added bonus. Refer to Chapter 4 on résumés for more examples of academics, awards and honors (academic and non-academic) extracurricular activities, and community service.

Essay-Based Scholarships

There are many scholarships that are based solely on an essay or may be the determining factor in similar applications. Almost all scholarship applications have an essay question, even if it's only a paragraph long. For seniors, these essays usually focus on your personal thoughts and come from the heart, rather than a research report. The most common question is: "What are your education and career goals?" The answer for this can be anywhere from 100 to 500 words, depending on the application. The importance of helping others is the next

most commonly asked question. Other topics include "Service above Self," "How can one person make a difference?" and "Why is volunteering important?" All these questions are basically the same essay, just reworded. Another common essay topic is writing about a person or event that has made an impact on your life, which is another prompt that's based on your opinion.

Some scholarships require an essay only. Anyone can apply for these. They do not require a certain GPA, community service, or extracurricular activities, which is great for many students. Some may involve a little research, but most for seniors at least, are just commonsense, opinionated essays. There are even some that ask for an essay that you may have previously used on a college application. Other scholarships want to know about the student's career choice, how he or she is getting there and why he or she chose it, or even why education is important. There have been essays on how a realtor helps his community, how fire sprinklers help, or even on any topic that is important to the student. These scholarships are perfect for students who have lower GPAs or have to work and have no time for community service or extracurricular activities to boost their resume.

Most students don't enjoy writing essays, especially prompts that require extra work. If the question makes it necessary for you to read a book or do research for the essay, the competition is cut way down and opens up the door for more chances to win.

Writing from the heart is usually the most important aspect in writing essays. More information on how to write an essay is located in Chapter 7.

Financial-Need Scholarships

There are scholarships mainly based on financial need, according to the parents' or guardians' income. Some are based only on income, such as the Pell Grant from FAFSA (see Chapter 10), while others ask about extenuating circumstances, which can vary. If the application asks for copies of a parent's W1040 or Student Aid Report from FAFSA, then it will be income based. However, extenuating circumstances can be a variety of different situations, such as a change in one of the parents' jobs (unemployment, less hours, or changing to an occupation with less income), separation or divorce, extra medical bills, or maybe a grandparent or another family member recently moved in with you. Those situations fall under unusual financial circumstances or financial need with circumstances. The situation could also be school costs and types of education (two years versus six or more and public schools versus private schools), and these can also count toward a student's need. Perhaps your parents just refuse to help finance any of your college education. Another factor could be that your parents make too much to receive any grants but not enough to pay for your college costs. No matter which category you fall into, you need to notify the scholarship committee about your financial situation.

There are also those applications that look at financial need but only count it as a small percentage of the overall picture. For example, if the student has high credentials in other areas, such as community service and grades, this may outweigh the financial-need criteria. I have seen students who didn't really have as much financial need as others win because they had higher points in other areas.

There is also the Free Application for Federal Student Aid (FAFSA) for students going to college based only on family and the student's income (this is discussed more in Chapter 10).

Scholarships for Minorities

Minority scholarships vary. Some are for individual minorities only, and others for African Americans, Hispanics, Native Indians, and Asians. The most common minority scholarships are for African Americans and Hispanics, and there are even a few that exclude Asians as a minority. However, Asians are becoming included more each year. There are also several scholarships for Native Americans, but Indian tribes disperse those (and you usually have to have a Tribal Card for proof to apply). Students can go online to find their tribe's official site and contact them about becoming a member. Just don't wait until your senior year to do this because time might be a factor in receiving your membership. On most minority scholarships, unless specified, you do not have to be 100 percent of that ethnic group to qualify.

Most of these scholarships are found online, but many local ones come from different organizations or even ones for certain majors. There are several African American sororities, fraternities, and organizations in my town that offer scholarships for the females and/or males and a local NAACP that offers them also. There is an American-Spanish Club that has scholarships for Hispanic students only. The community college even has one for the African  American student with the highest GPA from each high school in our county, and one for African American males who major in education. Most universities offer minority scholarships, but mainly for African American or Hispanic students.

There are scholarship applications that are for minorities only because there's a greater need for those types of employees in specific career fields. There are even some for females of any race because the glass ceiling is still there. It's best to put your race on your official transcripts to prove your heritage, even if the student is only 1/8 of that particular ethnicity.

One of the most common misconceptions when searching for minority scholarships is thinking that the search site will only bring up scholarships for minority students. Unfortunately, this is not the case, unless the website is NAACP or Hispanic Scholarship Funds. Scholarships usually found via Internet search are usually for any race. It takes patience and time to sift through them. You should use all related words when you google these scholarships, such as Hispanic or Latino, African American or Black, and Indian as well as Native American. But minority students shouldn't just apply for minority scholarships. Many students only want minority- or major-based scholarships. They should apply for every scholarship they are eligible for because there are so many different ones for all races or majors. The more you apply for, the better chance you have to win.

Scholarships for Specific Majors

There are many scholarships based on the student's planned major. The word "planned" is used because many students change their majors in college (some before they even start), but everyone must start off with a planned major, at least for most scholarship applications. The most common essay question is about education and career goals. Even if a student is not completely sure about which major to choose, he or she must have one career choice that interests him or her. Many students tell me that they have no idea; I respond by asking, *if you could be anything in the career world today, what would you be?* Most students do not choose something unrealistic (such being singer in a band when they are tone deaf), and the question actually gives them some ideas. If they are still clueless, I make them take a career-interest survey (which they previously did with me in the 9th or 10th grade) or google different career choices to examine requirements, education, or pay. I also suggest that they find some possible career choices that interest them through shadowing various occupations. If it is a position that is difficult to shadow, then try to contact someone in that profession, by email or telephone, and ask if they can talk to you or just answer some questions about their career.

The earlier a student picks a major, the sooner he or she can earn an undergraduate degree for the least amount of money. At some colleges, you can actually start taking classes toward your major during the first two years in place of electives. But changing your major halfway through college costs you time and money. If you switch your major to a completely different subject during your junior or senior year, you will have to backtrack and take more classes, adding another costly year or two onto your college costs. So try to explore all your options before your junior year in college through research, interning, or volunteering in different fields that interest you.

Scholarships that require enrolling into a specific major are usually from companies or organizations that specialize in that particular field. Jobs may even be offered to scholarship winners, upon graduation or as internships. Most companies will never even see the student, but sometimes they host award ceremonies for the winners. Typically, they don't keep tabs on students who've won. So if this is the case, then changing your major later down the road will not affect your scholarship. However, there are a few scholarships that are renewable while the student is in college, as long as the major stays the same. Using your major can come in handy in another way, but that will be discussed in Chapter 3.

Unique or Unusual Scholarships

There are also "unusual" scholarships that everyone talks about. Unfortunately, no one knows what they're called or how to find them. For example, there is a scholarship for left-handed people. I have had so many students and parents ask about this unique scholarship. A college representative even talked about it during a presentation, but no one, not even the representative, could tell me what the name of the scholarship was so I could search for it—they only knew it existed. I looked all over on the Internet and in scholarship books, but

I still couldn't find it. Through all the different scholarship search programs I've used, I've never come across a question asking about which hand you use. Finally, after much research, I came across it at the public library. Unfortunately, the scholarship was only for a particular college in

Pennsylvania, which meant a student had to attend that school to qualify. Yes, there are probably many unusual scholarships out there (I have yet to find the one that requires having two different-colored eyes), but these are most likely under very special circumstances.

There are also many organizations that have their own scholarships that some will find unusual, such as the Stuck at Prom Duct Tape Scholarship or the Florida Peanut Producers. You must own a peanut business to be eligible for the company's scholarship. If scholarships are too unique, then this means that most people are ineligible. Perhaps there is a left-handed club out there somewhere that may have a scholarship for any college, but for the most part, the odd ones are for very special circumstances only, and some, I believe, are just myths.

Your Scholarship Folder

Before you enter high school, start a folder that pertains to your academic and extracurricular achievements. Keep track of anything that seems important and update the folder throughout high school.

Remember to keep records of everything you are involved in, which begins the summer after eighth grade. Keep a list or copy of all your awards (academic and non-academic), extracurricular activities, and community service/volunteer work hours. Having copies of service hours can also come in handy if someone loses them for documentation purposes. I have seen this time and time again because we all make mistakes. You should also keep any well-written essays because you never know when you can use it for a scholarship application. Always have any special memories in mind and perhaps write something down about it in case you forget about it later on. If a specific event or moment impacted you or others, this can usually be used for an essay down the road. Students tend to forget about inspiring moments within a year or two, so it's important to save it. It could even be used on a college essay. You should also keep copies of your completed scholarship (and college) applications and letters of recommendations as well. Any copies of recent report cards and official transcripts can go in here, too.

Here is a list of items to keep in your folder:

- Any essays that are well written and personal
- Any impacting events in your life
- All community service hours, starting in the summer before ninth grade
- Documents of clubs, organizations, sports, and school involvement or committees
- Grades: honors, AP, or IB classes, a list of classes taken
- Special awards: academics (Student of the Year, etc.) and non-academics (such as sports and volunteer work) or anything else
- Letters of recommendation
- Copies of any completed applications (scholarship or college)
- Yearly academic histories, such as final report cards, print-outs from your guidance counselor and an extra copy of an official transcript, just in case you cannot get one for any last-minute applications

Apply and apply; again and again. If you aren't sure about eligibility requirements, call a contact number (which is usually on the application). I have even seen a scholarship from a music-singing club have no applicants, so they accepted instrument players. If you are close, it may be acceptable. You never know unless you ask. Apply for as many as you possibly can, whenever you can.

Chapter 3:

SEARCHING FOR SCHOLARSHIP APPLICATIONS

Your High School

The first place to look for scholarships is at your school. If you do not have a scholarship coordinator at your school, go to your senior guidance counselor. Many applications, or information regarding scholarship applications, are sent  directly to the guidance office, especially local ones. Applying to local scholarships doesn't mean you have to attend a local college to win them; the scholarship itself is given out locally, usually to students from high schools in a particular county. Regrettably, most guidance counselors do not have time to work on finding scholarships because of all their other paperwork, and many applications are either put aside or lost in the shuffle of papers. You can always make your own copy if there is only a master copy, and let them know that you are really interested in applying to scholarships. Unfortunately, if your school does not receive this information, you will need to track it down yourself. Go to your local school board and see what they can tell you. There is usually a department that's received scholarship information, such as guidance and testing or school activities. Go online to your county's school board website and search, also. You need to read local newspapers and listen to radio and television commercials as well. I've seen many local scholarships advertised that way.

Local Organizations/Clubs (Civic and Private)

Many local organizations love to assist students. There are so many different clubs in your area that give scholarships away. Some good examples would be any local club in your community, such as the Women's Club, the Elks Club, Lions Club, Rotary Club, Exchange Club, Daughters of the American Republic, or any other civic clubs (such as sororities or fraternities, or college alumni) in your area. Check with your nearest VFW posts because they always have different scholarship contests. Your local American Legion will also have various scholarships available. Look up organizations in your phone book and start calling around. Ask your parents, grandparents, or even parents of your friends, as many organizations also have scholarships for the members' children and sometimes grandchildren. I repeat, you will never know unless you ask.

Local Businesses/Stores/Churches

Many companies provide scholarships for students who major in their field, such as engineering, medical, or even pharmacy degrees. Some even want students to come back and work for them after graduation. I've found scholarships from different stores such as Wal-Mart, Target, Best Buy, Sears, JC Penney, and even local malls. Many provide scholarships for employees' children or even just for employees themselves, such as Wal-Mart, Target, or Chick-Fil-A. Not only do many of those companies help their own employees out, but they also give back to the community as well.

Whether it's at your parents' work or your own, ask the manager or owner about scholarships for employees. If they do not know anything about scholarships, call the head corporation. Keep asking until you get a definitive answer.

Church is another good place to check (as long as you are an active member) for scholarships, and many also have low-rate loans for members. Ask the minister or contact the main chapter of the church. I have even found several scholarships through various electric or utility companies for their customers and or employees. You need to look everywhere.

Websites

One of the best resources is the Internet. There are many scholarship searches that require you to fill out a questionnaire or personal profile so it can find scholarships that match your eligibility. Some excellent sites are **Scholarships.com**, **Fastweb.com**,  and **ScholarshipExperts.com**. (See Chapter 12 for more websites). You can always look for these online yourself to find even more. Just make sure that you NEVER pay someone to search for you. There are too many free scholarships out there. I had one student pay $40 for a search, and she brought me the results. I had most of them already through free searches. There were only about five new ones, but two of those scholarships no longer even existed.

Many scholarships are either a one-time deal, no longer available, or cancelled because committees have run out of funding or channeled their money toward other services such as the Sam Walton (Wal-Mart) or Target community scholarships. They still have scholarships for employees or their children, but both now use their money for other community projects.

There will always be scholarships that you'll be ineligible for when you use a scholarship search site. My daughter, a protestant and Florida resident, majored in education, and her search found a scholarship for education majors who were Jewish and lived in New York. The common factor, education, pulled the scholarship up. I have also seen a profile match students who will be freshmen in college with a scholarship just for graduate students only. It can take just one factor to match you up with an irrelevant scholarship, so patience is required. When you search for scholarships, read all the eligibility requirements before applying, and you will save yourself much time. Remember to look at the deadline. Sometimes scholarships are discontinued or simply no longer available. I've found that many websites take you to expired applications. You can also simply google scholarships by major, city, state, or other requirements. As with any type of website search, you need to look for these under a variety of words or descriptions.

The downfall of scholarship search results is that most are national scholarships, which means there's a wider applicant pool. Remember that the competition is much harder because you are competing against more students. Yes, it is possible to win a national scholarship, but you need to have a strong background in the required eligibility. My son applied for an online national athletic/academic scholarship, which I thought he would have a fairly good chance at winning because he played sports full time for four years and excelled in them. Then we found out that 76,000 other students also applied for the same scholarship. Many more students seem to apply when the Internet is involved.

You can also do manual searches yourself either at your local or school library, and they will usually have scholarship books in their research section. The only problem is that many scholarships are no longer available depending on how recently the books were published. I have seen scholarships that have been around for a long time, ones that are only around for a year or two, and some that return again after being gone. Because the economy has been down over the past several years, some of the oldest scholarships are slowly dropping out or finding other avenues to donate money. Make sure to check the deadline: date and year.

If you need to write and request an application, make sure you send a self-addressed and stamped envelope. Sometimes it's required, but even if it isn't, putting one in there just makes it easier for them to send the application to you.

Your College's Financial Aid Office

Another excellent source for finding scholarships is your college. Call the financial aid office and pick up a list of scholarships and application deadlines; go online and search as well. Many colleges also have scholarships within the programs you are majoring in. There are also privately funded (sometimes called foundation) scholarships that are for a particular school but are funded through individuals or businesses. You should use different variations of words when searching, such as scholarships for the name of the college, or private or foundation scholarships (or awards) for University of _____.

Don't give up after your freshman year if you don't receive any scholarships. Try every year you are there. One of my former students told me that he has won quite a few since being in college because there was less competition.

Another student visited the financial aid department on a weekly basis after school started. On her third or fourth visit, she was rewarded for her persistence. They gave her a $1,000 scholarship that someone else received but never attended the school to receive it. Do not give up!

Many colleges have automatic scholarships for incoming students based on GPA and test scores (and many of these are renewable if you maintain a certain GPA). I always tell my students to apply early because some scholarships are based on first come, first serve. However, there is a chance for you to be awarded one of the freshman scholarships if you bring up your test scores. One student finally bumped up her test scores during April of her senior year after she had already been accepted. She emailed the financial aid office, notified them about her higher test scores and asked if they had any unclaimed scholarships left. This email paid off her efforts—she won $8,000 over the course of four years. Never be afraid to ask.

Remember to call your state's financial aid office about any scholarships or grants they have for instate residents attending public or private colleges (see Chapter 10).

Chapter 4:
CREATING A FOUR-PURPOSE RÉSUMÉ

My students visit my room twice a year, starting in ninth grade. In journal form, they start working on their résumés by listing awards, extracurricular activities, community service, and work experience. At the end of their junior year or beginning of their senior year, students turn it into a professional résumé.

Essentially, there are four ways to create and use a great resume. Students can use them for four different purposes: college applications, scholarship applications, letters of recommendation, and job applications. Creating a résumé is the key tool for filling out scholarship applications. I'll go over how to apply them to everyday life in Chapter 6, but this chapter focuses on creating the best resume.

Your basic résumé templates are located on most office programs, such as Microsoft Word. Some scholarship applications ask for only a résumé instead of an essay. After creating a résumé, it's beneficial to take the same format and replicate it into a blank document because a majority of applications will ask questions in a variety of ways. My cut-and-paste method is best used for these types of applications. This method works best when it's not on a program's template; it's user-friendly. Refer to Chapter 6 for more information on shortcut methods.

A résumé should be brief and only list important details. Do not use pronouns or write lengthy descriptions. People, as a rule, generally do not like to read long passages and only want to read the best things about you. If they get bored because it is too long, they might skim over what you put down and will miss important information.

At the end of this chapter is a sample résumé. Take that same information and set it up to use for my shortcut method.

Basic Resume Outline

Your basic résumé starts with the header: your name, street address, telephone, and email information. Then the objective comes next.

Objective

The "objective" section is the top subject. This can vary, depending on what you are using the résumé for. If a scholarship application requests a copy of your résumé, then the objective would be the same as a college résumé. For example: "Planning to major in (insert major)." You can omit this section if you want; it's optional.

Work Experience

If you're using your résumé for job applications, then work experience would be the next topic. However, if you are using it for a scholarship or college application, then work experience should go last. People like to see that students are already trying to help themselves or their families.

Work experience should be listed from present to past. You should have the starting date, the ending date (or put "present", if still there), the name of the company, your job title, and a brief description of what you do. Once again, leave out first-person pronouns to make it brief. Put down examples that display leadership skills, such as being in charge of a specific job or other employees. Also, list any accolades, such as "Employee of the Month" or other awards and promotions.

If you left a job under a bad situation or only stayed a short time, don't list it. One of my students was fired for theft (but not arrested) and claimed that he was wrongly accused. Even though he was probably telling the truth, he still wanted to list that job. Thankfully, I talked him out of it because you cannot defend yourself in a résumé. If the topic came up in an interview, then that would be the time to discuss what actually happened, if you felt that it was necessary.

Academics (for scholarship applications) or Education (for work applications)

"Academics" is the next subject. Scholarship and college applications are only interested in your high school years. First, list the name of your school, projected graduation date, and then academic honors. You can start with your graduation status if it's excellent. Typically, an honors degree is between a 3.0 to 3.49, 3.50 to 4.0 for high honors, and 4.0 and above is highest honors. A student with a 3.5 GPA could write: "graduating with high honors," or if you hope to have a 3.5 by the time you graduate, you could put: "plan to graduate with high honors."

If your GPA is not high but you've at least been on the honor roll, you could put down "honor roll"—even that sounds good. Of course, if your GPA is low, then just leave it out. Next, list all honors, Advanced Placement, ACE, International Baccalaureate, or dual enrollment classes because these classes have rigorous, challenging curriculum. These classes are taken into consideration. Don't list each one separately. Instead, put: "various honors and AP classes – 4 years", or "all academic honors classes – 4 years."

Next, list any academic type organizations you belong to. These types of clubs usually require a certain grade criteria to receive an invitation to join, such as the National Honor Society. Students can also list items such as the academic math club, Mu Alpha Theta, or Academic Team. If a club invited you to join but you didn't, you could write: "National Honor Society – nominee."

Always list the number of years of membership. If you've belonged to a club for only a year, you can omit this, as it is taken for granted. You should also put down, under the organization, any offices you held or any awards you won from them.

List any other academic awards you received. Some examples would be a math award, Student of the Year award, faculty-selected award (even citizenship awards), or leadership and college summer programs you've attended. If you were selected for the same award more than once, you'd write: "Multiple Honoree." You should always list the most important awards first, with nominee awards last.

Always list vocational classes you took for two or more years if they pertain to your major. This shows the scholarship committee that you are serious about your career choice; the panelists will, most likely, want to put their money to good use. For example: teacher assistantships, art, drafting, cabinet making, business classes, auto mechanics, criminal justice, health occupations, or even extra academic classes, such as the sciences, if you are planning on pursuing that field are good ones to use.

Extracurricular Activities

Extracurricular activities is the next section. This can be filled out in one of two ways: you can list clubs (or any organization) that you belong to, along with sports; or if you have a long history in sports, "sports" can be its own section. Once again, this time frame begins with high school. You can actually start the summer before ninth grade because you technically are a freshman after eighth grade graduation.

Always put down the number of years you've participated in any given activity. If you were an officer, captain of a team, or on a varsity team, list that, too (remember, these are also examples of leadership). You would add any other awards you received from different organization in this section. For sports, this includes awards and certificates such as "the most valuable player" or "most improved player". If your team (or just you) won any championships, this would go here, too, listing the most important or highest level first. Remember that being an officer, captain, or on a varsity team are types of non-academic awards, as well as leadership skills.

Be sure to list your most participated activity first, or the most meaningful one, then finish with the smallest amount or least time of membership. If you put clubs and sports together under extracurricular, keep the lists separate. Again, put the one that you have the most experience with first.

Let us say you listed clubs first. It's always a good idea to put down your school-involved organizations first, and then list the community (or outside of school) ones.

Student council and government are great organizations to be involved in. Even though they aren't really considered a club, they are very active organizations. Even the 'Butterfly Club' would be an organization that would count, as long as you attend meetings and do whatever you do (catch, classify, etc.) with butterflies. Do not, however, list anything twice on your résumé or a scholarship application. Keep National Honor Society under Academics or, in a scholarship application, under academic awards. But do not list it again under extracurricular activities.

Sports can be done a little differently. Always put the school team first, but if you were involved with the same sport in a city league, list the school sport then the same sport outside of school before moving onto a completely different sport. (See my résumé sample under sports.)

Think about different types of organizations you belonged to. Include church membership, church youth groups or choir, any clubs, any sports, Explorers, 4H, Girl Scouts or Boy Scouts, and even any types of lessons you've taken (i.e. music, dance, acting). You should also list any camps or conventions you have attended under that particular sport, club, or organization. Band and ROTC can also be listed, as long as you have extra hours outside of the classroom, because they also show commitment.

All these show an involvement in something that you have done or are doing on your own time. Scholarship committees love to see that a student is involved in something outside the classroom.

If you are no longer involved in any club or sport, put it down anyway. Yes, the longer the involvement the better, but on the other hand, a little is better than none. However, you must belong for a full school year (unless membership started half way through) to count it. If you quit in the middle of a season or school year, you cannot count it.

Community Service

The next subject on the résumé is community service, also known as volunteer work or involvement. This is where you might list a club or organization a second time if you have service hours with them. Some students volunteer at their school, others in the community, and many even go on mission trips to other states or countries with their churches or other organizations. Wherever you volunteer, whatever you do, keep track of your involvement and hours. Most scholarships prefer service for nonprofit organizations, but many still look at other types of volunteering. For example, if you work at a doctor's office or vet's office, it's not typically considered community service and should be listed under extracurricular. Just make sure you add 'volunteer' hours. However if it's a clinic for the needy, then it's considered community service. Because you don't know what each individual scholarship panel is looking for (unless it's specifically stated), make sure you include everything on the application.

You really need to count up all the hours you've helped someone or an organization. Remember you cannot include family, or even neighbors, unless you are helping your neighbors with an organization, such as your church. Ask your parents to look over your activities and hours because they may remember more than you. Once again, include any planning you've done, such as preparing for Sunday school class, managing your club or a school dance. You should also include the time it took you to

travel to the volunteer site, as long as it is local. It's all part of the free time you gave up to help someone or a cause.

Each county, state, or even school accepts different types of community service hours. If you're not sure about what they recognize, then you should call your local school board office to find out what is acceptable to include as community hours. For example, one school in my district wouldn't let the students use service hours at the hospital if they worked in the gift shop. My school, however, allows students to use that as community service hours because they are still helping the hospital, as well as assisting families and patients. Hospitals and nursing homes, even if they are for-profit businesses, can be used because no matter what task the student does, they are still helping needy people in some way.

As with extracurricular activities, list the service that you have the most hours in first. If it's not obvious what you did because just listing the place where you volunteered is not enough, then briefly explain what the service was. You also need to remember to put down the hours spent next to the activity. You may have "band performance for nursing homes," but if you do not put down hours, it looks like you only did it once or twice. This is very important for any application, whether its scholarship or college admissions related.

Once again, there are two ways to list your hours. You can either put down the total amount of hours or how many hours weekly/monthly and how many years you have done it. Just remember that, if you list your hours the second way (weekly or monthly), you also need to have the number of weeks, months, or years you were involved. If you put "worked three hours a week" but forget the years, it sounds like you might have just volunteered once or twice. If you put the number of years without the hours, it once again sounds like you only did it once or twice.

However, there may be different types of volunteer activities you've only spent a few hours on. I would group anything less than 10 hours total together with similar activities. Perhaps you volunteered at an elementary school's carnival, helped at an open house, and tutored students but served only two or three hours at a time. Add them up and put them under "various local elementary school events", and list the activities under it. If you volunteered a few hours at a wide range of dissimilar organizations, you could add up all those hours and put them under "various community service activities", then list the activities beneath that.

But if it's a very isolated service that you do not have anything to combine it with, such as a club that requires new members to visit a nursing home only twice, I would list this as, "nursing home visits," and leave it at that.

Once again, any planning, organizing, or leading meetings also count toward service hours, just as the travel time to get there does, too. You can list tasks such as "tutoring students for free" only if there is an adult who can confirm that. Unfortunately, helping an elderly neighbor, does not count, but you can still list it under extracurricular activities if you so desire.

I would also include any unpaid community performances, such as a play, singing, or even instrumental events. My school's band members have to perform at football games, which cannot be counted as community service because it's a part of their grade. But when they march in the Christmas parade or perform at graduation, they can count those hours as well as practices for those performances as community service. You can also include helping a teacher in his or her classroom or just helping to clean up the school, as long as it's outside of normal school hours. You can use hours for working at concession stands, keeping score for any sport, or even recording statistics for a sport.

But, once again, if you have performed community service as a requirement from the judge or court, you can't include this on a scholarship or college application because you didn't volunteer to perform the task.

There are many clubs that require a certain number of hours of service per month from their members. My club requires two hours a month, but the officers and many members volunteer much more than that. When listing this on an application or résumé, they should write the name of the club, how many hours of service they have per month (the required hours only), and how many years they have done this. Many students, and most officers, volunteer beyond the required amount of hours. This is when they should list any extra hours spent on a particular project under a separate topic. For example, the student might have spent 20 hours on one project in a single month even though the club only required two hours of service that month. So he or she would list the 18 extra hours under the name of the project. Many scholarship committees want to see students more involved than completing just the required hours.

Fundraisers serve as another type of community service, as long as the raised money is for a non-profit charity or organization. List which organization you're raising the money for and why it's a worthwhile cause (such as Red Cross for hurricane victims, money for scholarships, or money for needy families during the holidays). You don't always receive hours for fundraisers at some schools and isn't usually counted toward community service if the funds are used to buy uniforms or equipment for a team or the band. However, it's still worth mentioning because raising money for any cause still shows a commitment on your behalf.

You also need to include any awards or special recognition you received for community service hours under the activity. List this under the volunteer activity itself. It's also a type of non-academic award, which I will give more examples of in Chapter 6. These awards seem to be harder to come by, so if you are in a club that does community service, it's worthwhile to talk to your sponsor to see if he or she can award a certificate for a certain number of volunteer hours. Potential awards are also a great incentive for getting more students involved.

You need to keep track of anything and everything that you do as you do it. Four years may seem like a short amount of time, but many students have a difficult time remembering everything they did just two or three years ago.

I've included a sample résumé for you on the next page. But you'll need to refer to Chapter 6 to see how I set up each section for my quick and easy way to fill out multitudes of scholarship applications.

Mark J. Lane

1234 NE Any Street
Anywhere, FL 11111
Phone (555) 555-5555

Objective: Planning to major in Architecture

Work Experience: 06/13-present   Painter's Paradise   Ocala, FL
Painter's Apprentice - two separate businesses
- Prep and paint interiors and exteriors and pressure clean

Academics: Graduation 06/16   Vanguard High School   Ocala, FL
Will graduate with High Honors (this student has not yet graduated)
National Honors Society - 2 years
- Historian

Florida Top 20 Scholars
All Honors/AP Academic classes-4 years
Biology Award-Student of the Year
Academic Team-3 years

Extracurricular Activities: VHS Football Team - 4 years
- Varsity - 2 years
- Super Knight Award - 2 years
- Summer work-out camp - 4 years

VHS Wrestling Team - 2 years
- Varsity -2 years
- Captain - 1 year
- State Finalist-1 year
- Regional Champion-1 year (Semi Finalist-1 year)
- Marion County Champion -2 years

USA Wrestling – 2 years
VHS Baseball Team - 2 years
Student Government Representative - 4 years
Interact Service Club - 2 years
Anchor Service Club - Elected Sweetheart

Community Service: Vanguard High School Volunteer - 3 years - 110- hours
- Assisted office personnel with school start and ending

Anchor Service Club T-Bird - 1.5 years - 4 hrs. monthly (not required)
- Help the homeless
- Assist with adopting a highway and clean up litter

Bible School Aide - 20 hours
Warm-up Ocala Campaign for homeless and needy - 20 hours

Chapter 5:

BASIC RULES FOR FILLING OUT APPLICATIONS

Neatness is extremely important when filling out an application. There are even some scholarships that have a preliminary elimination process, and sloppy applications are tossed out solely for that reason. Always type up your application, but if there's no possible way to do this, then write carefully in your best handwriting. When you make a mistake, start over. If it's not possible to start fresh, use a small amount of Wite-Out®. Remember to never cross off mistakes because this makes your application appear messy. Presentation represents you. Uncluttering and simplifying your application makes panelists want to read it more thoroughly.

While organization is important, having correct grammar, punctuation, and spelling is more vital. For a scholarship committee, it's difficult to choose a winner because there are many well-qualified applications to pick from. Using proper grammar and spelling could make your application stand out. I've met people who won't even consider an application if there's bad grammar or misspelled words. You should always proofread your application for any mistakes and have a parent or another adult proofread as well. Always ask for help.

Just remember, a computer's spellcheck doesn't correct every grammar or spelling mistake.

Another important aspect to keep in mind is reading all the application's directions. If the application asks for black ink, then use black ink; don't use a pencil or blue ink. Some applications only accept typed documents, whereas others prefer hand-written essays. Sometimes, just one mistake disqualifies you from the competition. So when you take the time to complete your application, do it well.

Always read the instructions carefully. Many applications have similar questions but not necessarily in the same order. Examples of similar questions are used in my cut-and-paste method located in Chapter 6. Make sure you understand essay questions and give the correct answer. Do not stray from the subject. Chapter 7 goes more in-depth about writing essays.

Make sure that any extra attachments are included with the application, such as letters of recommendation or official transcripts. Some scholarship applications want a transcript and copy of your most recent report card. Even though your grades are on your transcripts, send both if required. There are even some that want attachments stapled in a certain corner or require you to put your name on the application in a particular way or place. Some don't even want any attachments.

Reading the directions is the difference between winning and losing. Never leave a question unanswered, but if you do, make sure that it's something that isn't applicable to you. While proofreading, you might discover that you accidentally left an answer blank. A student several years ago was highly qualified for a particular scholarship that was worth $20,000. When he found out that one of his friends, who was less qualified than him, was a semi-finalist and he wasn't, we all wondered why. When I called, I discovered that even though the application was for seniors only and had a senior guidance counselor's signature, he left one of the easiest questions on the application blank: "What grade are you in?" The computer threw him out because he skipped that question. If you find that you left a question blank, you might need to practice your proofreading skills.

I can't stress this next rule enough: **do not** send in the application late because deadlines are extremely important. This is just another way to get thrown out. Unless the application asks for a "postmark", assume the deadline date is when the committee wants to receive the

application. I have students' mail their applications at least a week ahead of the due date. I've mailed two different items at the same time and to the same city. One parcel arrived there the next day, whereas the other took five days. After doing all that work, it would be such a waste to get disqualified just because your application was late. If you're not sure about the deadline, contact someone to find out more information. For example, I recently received an application where the deadline read, 'postmark by February 15 but also stated, "Make sure we receive it by February 15." A postmark means that a parcel needs to be in the mail by a specific date (usually by 5 p.m.), so these instructions contradicted each other. I called and cleared up the error, but if you don't find a correct answer or are unable to call, then have your application there by the earliest deadline (in this case, mail early enough to be received by February 15).

Many scholarship applications are now available online and sometimes can only be filled out this way. Send these applications in early just in case you have computer or Internet problems (or if their website has glitches). You can always go to your public library or school library if your computer messes your application up. One student applied to a scholarship online that was due that day but found out that she needed a letter of recommendation. It wasn't in the general requirements, but just a random request at the end of the application. Unfortunately, she waited too late to apply for this scholarship. Always read instructions ahead of time, even for online applications. Many applications request that you complete part of the application online and send hard copies of documents by mail. The deadlines might even differ. Remember that there is no spell check when answering an essay question online. It's better to write out the question on a Microsoft Office® Word document (or whatever program you use) and then check for spelling yourself as well. After proofreading, copy and paste your answer onto the online application. You can even save your answer for future reference when you use this method.

There are a few exceptions where late applications might still be accepted. I've seen several local scholarships extend their deadlines over the years; it just depends on how many applications the committee received. Some applicants have extenuating circumstances and bring their applications in late because of emergencies. I usually call the scholarship panelists, and sometimes they allow students to drop them off or mail them late because of this. It never hurts to ask—but always give your best effort to complete and send in the application early.

There are times when a student runs close to the deadline but there are a few options to expedite his or her application. He or she can choose priority mail, which is relatively inexpensive, and will usually get the application there in a day or two, or overnight it, but this is more expensive. If it's a local scholarship, then students can actually drop it off themselves, as long as there is a physical address. It's always a good idea to make sure they know you're coming and where they want you to drop off the application. Make sure you leave your application in a waterproof package (zip-lock baggie or even a plastic grocery bag), because rain or other liquid elements can ruin your application. However, some scholarships only have a post-office box address, so they are near impossible to drop off unless you have the correct post office and a helpful employee. Several of my students have actually gone to the post office and asked someone to personally put the letter in the box on the day it was due, and their application was accepted.

When applying for scholarships, find out information about the contest's judges or organization. Of course, this is impossible to do for every single scholarship application, but focus on a few that are harder or more selective. For example, the VFW (Veterans of Foreign Wars) has an essay contest every year, and the members are judges. These committee panelists are older, patriotic people who dedicated years of service for their country. Appeal to their sentimental, patriotic emotions. If a company gives out a scholarship for their area of expertise, focus on the company's accomplishments, quality work and integrity.

Many community clubs have scholarships. See what they focus on and what type of service it is. You can usually relate your essay to the organization. For example, if a church is giving out a scholarship, you need to include any church participation and/or service activities in the application or essay. If the club has a motto or creed, try to relate your essay to it, if possible.

When you think you're done, double-check everything one last time. Make a copy of every application in case an interview comes up or to use it again on a different scholarship application. One student called me in a panic because she received a call requesting an interview. She wasn't sure which application it was for because the name of the scholarship was in remembrance of a former member, not the name of the organization. Luckily, I was familiar with this scholarship and knew that it was the Lions Club. She found her application copy and was able to prepare for questions. Even though the essay question was mainly about her major, her volunteer work stood out. She had worked with a young blind girl and taught her how to cheerlead with other girls. This experience strongly impacted her because she enjoyed helping the little girl feel like she belonged; that she was the same as everyone else for a change. She learned that the Lions Club helped the blind, and so she planned on talking about her experience at the interview. Chapter 7 will go more in-depth about knowing your audience.

Make sure to double-check all minor and major details in your essay and that your answers are relevant. Three of my students applied for over fifteen scholarships each and didn't win one of them. One student wrote in every career goal essay that she wanted to be a lawyer. She later found out that her sealed letter of recommendation from her guidance counselor (which she used for almost every application) said that she'd make a great doctor. This was a definite miscommunication.

Another student had an abnormally large number of volunteer hours with his church because his father was the pastor. However, he didn't log any of these hours. Because they weren't confirmed on his transcripts, the amount of hours was unbelievable.

The third student didn't bring any of her applications to me until the end of the year, but told me that she filled them out exactly as I told her to. I finally convinced her to let me look over an application and discovered that she needed to proofread her essays and rewrite them. After working with her on a last few applications, she did win a scholarship. Hopefully, after reading this book, you will avoid mistakes like these.

Chapter 6:
SHORTCUTS FOR A FASTER AND EASIER APPLICATION PROCESS

A typed application always looks better than a handwritten one. They are neater, more professional, and easier to read. My shortcut method provides you with a nicely printed application that you don't need to retype every time you start new one. This method is for applicants who don't have a scanner or computer. Just recently, I've found programs you can download onto your computer and type directly on the application as if it was scanned to your email.

If you're unable to scan or download anything, you can use the old-fashioned method I used for my daughter that I will be going over in this chapter. She applied for a few scholarship applications early on, but started filling them out in earnest during her senior year. She applied to over 25 different scholarships. We found a way to fill them out in a speedy, assembly line-like manner with my shortcut method.

Many scholarships ask the same questions, just differently. I created a simple way for my daughter to implement her resources while taking shortcuts. She completed seven scholarships with this method in one night in just two hours (not counting essays).

Always have your résumé ready. As I previously mentioned in Chapter 4, retype your résumé without the template. Go to your résumé and transfer the information into a blank document. Transferring the data directly from the résumé is possible, but when you need to cut, copy, and paste, the template isn't user-friendly anymore. You can do it but it needs fixing along the way.

Start off with your work experience but use briefer information than you would for a normal résumé (in the work summary). Most questions ask about work experience and mainly want to know where you worked, how long you have been there, and how many hours you work per week. List them as you did on the résumé, from present to past.

The next section contains your academics. You can set this up like a résumé by putting all your academic awards and honors in this section (That is why I call this the academic awards section). Start with the most impressive awards because they will be read first. Then set them up in the same order as your résumé, with your extracurricular activities and community service sections following in pursuit.

After retyping your document, save it on a hard drive and flash drive, to be extra safe. Yes, this might be overly cautious but computers crash and flash drives go bad all the time. Something this important needs to be saved. Now that everything is typed, my shortcut method comes into play.

Some scholarship applications want academic awards separate from non-academic awards, whereas others ask for all awards. Other applications ask for school extracurricular activities and community extracurricular activities, while most combine all extracurricular activities into one question. Community service (volunteer hours) is usually the same. However, a few ask for community service and church activities separately. When an application asks for school and community activities and doesn't directly mention volunteer or community service anywhere on the application, then you would put your service hours under school or community activities depending where you did the service or if it's related to a school club or organization. Put any school-related activities (i.e. clubs, helping schools) under school activities and anything outside school, (i.e. church, helping the needy, Habitat for Humanities) under the community activities. Just make sure that actual community service (i.e. volunteering), along with the hours, goes somewhere on the application, even if you have to bring it up in your essay.

Below are some examples. They are a repeat of what I have already gone over with you, but repetition helps you remember what to include.

Academic Honors

Once again, here is where all your academic honors go, such as graduation (honors, high honors or even honor roll), National Honors Society, Mu Alpha Theta, or any other academic organizations you belong to. As stated before, this includes any academic awards you received, such as a math award, English award, or even a faculty-selected award (if based on grades). Include higher-level classes you took, such as honors, Advanced Placement, International Baccalaureate, AICE, or dual enrollment. If you belong to an academic team, list it here as well as any summer college programs you've attended.

Non-Academic Awards

This includes extracurricular and community service awards, such as holding an officer position (include any other positions here if they don't directly ask for them elsewhere), student government representative (senator), captain of a team, member on a varsity team, or even a volunteer award. If you were elected to be an officer, then write 'selected' after the position's title. Other awards include winning or placing in band or theater competitions and sports competitions at county level or higher. Always start with the highest award first. If you made it to the state finals but didn't place, start with "State Semi-Finalist" or "State Qualifier", then list the next highest level, with county last.

Sometimes, the application includes all of the above by asking for **academic and non-academic awards and honors** (or as colleges put it, "Talents/Honors and Awards") in one question. Then you would list all awards and honors from each category, both academic and non-academic. Just cut and paste to combine them.

If the application doesn't specifically ask for awards, make sure you still list them in their own category (i.e. captain or varsity member with the sport and officer with the organization).

Some applications separate activities. Below are some examples.

List all <u>school</u> activities.

This would include school-based clubs, sports, and any other school activities, including community service through your club or school (if there isn't a separate question for that).

List all <u>community</u> activities.

This includes clubs or sports not related to school and community service outside of your school (for example, if you volunteered at a school other than yours), unless there is a question specifically for community service.

After getting your information together, go to your blank document and type the name of the scholarship you are working on. This may seem like a silly thing to do, but if you are serious about winning and apply to an abundance of scholarships, organization keeps them separated. After that, type up each question as a heading. At the end of this chapter, I will use the résumé from Chapter 4, retype it for you, and highlight some of the examples I just went over. I will also show you some sample questions, so you can see where I actually put each answer.

After retyping your résumé, the cut-and-paste method comes in. If you have an application that asks for awards and honors as one question, list the scholarship, type "Awards and Honors," and cut and paste together from each category under this heading.

Now, for the old-fashioned method: Continue to answer each question like that and then print it. After printing, you'll cut out the answers with scissors. Place the cutout answers neatly on the application and use a small piece of tape to secure it. Do that for all of the questions. Then simply make a copy of the taped-up application, and you no longer see the tape. Sometimes, you will need to make your print smaller to fit into the section, or you can just cut your list in half and tape it, side by side, in columns.

But if you can add attachments, life becomes much easier. On a blank document, write the questions word-for-word under the headings, cut and paste the answers from your resume, print, and attach the entire paper to the application. Do not forget to print out "see attachment" by each question. Just remember that some applications don't want any attachments, so read the directions carefully. If you do attach a page, make sure you use the exact same format and order that the application has. You'll most likely need to cut and paste onto the computer copy to get it right. DO NOT print out the information in just any order (I cannot stress this enough). You must make sure your information is in the identical order and format that the application questions are.

Now, the application is almost finished, except for basic information: name, address, school you are attending, and any colleges you want to attend, etc. This can either be carefully handwritten or typed up on the computer, then print, hand-cut, taped, and copied just like you did on the answers.

If you have a scanner with the correct program, you can skip all of the above, scan the application, and type the answers on it. If you cannot type directly on the scanned application, there are programs on the Internet that you can download for free to enable you to do this. For the basic awards, extracurricular and community service questions, you can just cut and paste your information onto the application directly from your word document. For students who don't have a scanner or don't have a program that they can type directly on, my old-fashioned method can be used and cuts down on work and time. All of this saves you from typing the same information over and over again, especially when you have several scholarships due at the same time.

Because many scholarship applications are completed online, you really need to be careful. There are quite a few ways to accomplish this. Some want you to print the application, fill it out, and then put it in the mail, while others allow you to fill it out online but still want you to print it out and mail it with other attachments. I've also seen a few applications that ask you to submit the application online but want you to put transcripts and letters of reference in the mail. Be aware of deadlines because certain applications have the same submission date for online and mailed attachments. Of course, some organizations want everything submitted online. If you have any letters of recommendations, the writers need to know how to submit them properly. You can even offer to scan and send it for them, if needed. If they prefer or request to send it themselves, remind them before the deadline, and always make copies of everything. If you have attachments that need to be scanned and you don't have a scanner, you can usually find a friend or someone from your school that has one, and they can email it to you for you to submit. If you don't know anyone who has one, then most copy centers can scan it for you, possibly for a fee, but normally a low one.

Now, onto the essay portion of most applications: When you complete an essay, save it under the scholarship's section on your computer. An interview may come up, and you'll want to remember what you wrote the essay about for that particular scholarship (refer to Chapter 9 for more on interviews).

You'll find that you can reuse most essays by adding or subtracting from them. I will go into more detail about this in Chapter 7.

Sample Résumé (to transfer to a blank document)

Mark J. Lane

1234 NE Any Street
Ocala, FL 11111
Phone (555) 555-5555

Objective:	Planning to major in Architecture	
Work Experience:	06/13-present Painter's Paradise	Ocala, FL
	Painter's Apprentice - two separate businesses	
	• Prep and paint interiors and exteriors and pressure cleaning	
Academics:	Graduation 06/14 Vanguard High School	Ocala, FL
	Will graduate with High Honors (this student has not yet graduated)	
	National Honors Society - 2 years	
	• Historian	
	All Honors/AP Academic classes-4 years	
	Biology Award-Student of the Year	
	Academic Team-3 years	
	Florida Top 20 Scholars	
Extracurricular Activities	VHS Football Team - 4 years	
	• Varsity - 2 years	
	• Super Knight Award - 2 years	
	• Summer Work-Out Camp - 4 years	
	VHS Wrestling Team - 2 years	
	• Varsity-2 years	
	• Captain - 1 year	
	• State Finalist-1 year	
	• Regional Champion-1 year (Semi Finalist-I year)	
	• Marion County Champion -2 years	
	USA Wrestling — 2 years	
	VHS Baseball Team - 2 years	
	Student Government Representative - 4 years	
	Interact Service Club - 2 years	
	Anchor Service Club - Elected Sweetheart	
Community Service:	Vanguard High School Volunteer - 3 years - 110- hours	
	• Assisted office personnel with school start and ending	
	Anchor Service Club T-Bird - 1.5 years - 4 hrs. monthly (not required)	
	• Help the homeless	
	• Assist with adopting a highway and clean up litter	
	Bible School Aide - 20 hours	
	Warm-up Ocala Campaign for homeless and needy - 20 hours	

Type up similar to a résumé by starting with a blank document.

Work Experience:

06/13 – Present	Painters Paradise – Apprentice
06/11 – 05/13	Publix Supermarket – Cashier

Academics:

Will Graduate with High Honors
National Honors Society – 2 years
  • Historian
All Honors/AP classes – 4 years
Biology Award – Student of the Year
Academic Team – 3 years
Florida's Top 20 Scholars

Extracurricular Activities:

VHS Football Team – 4 years
  • Varsity – 2 years
  • Super Knight Award – 2 years
  • Summer Workouts – 4 years
VHS Wrestling Team – 2 years
  • Varsity – 2 years
  • Captain – 1 year
  • State Finalist – 1 year
  • Regional Champion – 1 year
  • Semi–Finalist – 1 year
  • Marion County Champion – 2 years

USA Wrestling Team – 2 years
VHS Baseball Team – 2 years
Student Government Representative (elected) – 4 years
Interact Service Club – 2 years
Anchor Service Club Sweetheart (elected) – 2 years

Community (Volunteer) Service

Vanguard High School Volunteer – 3 years –110+ hours
  • Assisted various office personnel with school start and ending
Anchor Service Club Sweetheart – 1.5 years – 4 hours monthly
(not required)
  • Help the homeless
  • Assist with adopting a highway and clean up litter
Bible School Aide – 20 hours
Warm-up Ocala Campaign for the homeless and needy – 20 hours

How you would cut and paste:

THE MARK MM SCHOLARSHIP

1. **List all your awards - both Academic and Non-Academic.**
   (This is where you will cut and paste all award-type answers – as I did below.)

Awards: Academic and Non-Academic

Will graduate with High Honors
National Honors Society – 2 years
  • Historian

All Honors/AP classes – 4 years
Biology Award – Student of the Year
Academic Team – 3 years
Florida's Top 20 Scholars
Football Awards:
- Varsity Football Team – 2 years
- Super Knight Award

Wrestling Awards:
- Varsity Wrestling Team – 2 years
- Captain Wrestling Team
- State Finalist – 1 year
- Regional Champion – 1 year
- Semi–Finalist –1 year
- Marion County Champion – 2 years

Student Government Representative (elected)
Anchor Sweetheart – 2 years (elected)

OR the question could be: **List all your Academic Awards**, and the next question could be **List all your Non-Academic Awards**. You would simply cut and paste the exact order that is used above. Below is an example.

Academic Awards:

Will graduate with High Honors
National Honors Society – 2 years
- Historian

All Honors/AP classes – 4 years
Biology Award-Student of the Year
Academic Team – 3 years
Florida's Top 20 Scholars

Non-Academic Awards:

Football Awards:
- Varsity Football Team – 2 years
- Super Knight Award

Wrestling Awards:
- Varsity Wrestling Team – 2 years
- Captain Wrestling Team
- State Finalist – 1 year
- Regional Champion – 1 year
- Semi–Finalist – 1 year
- Marion County Champion – 2 years

Student Government Representative (elected)

Anchor Sweetheart (elected) – 2 years

Don't leave out anything, no matter how insignificant. For example, under academic activities, there may be room for only five items, and the application doesn't want any attachments. You could put "historian" next to National Honors Society because you don't want to leave out leadership positions and add 'all honors/AP classes' next to 'will graduate with high honors'.

Example:

List Five Academic Awards:

- Will graduate with High Honors, with all Honors/AP classes – 4 years
- National Honors Society – 2 years – Historian
- Biology Award – Student of the Year
- Academic Team – 3 years
- Florida's Top 20 Scholars

Or the question could be: **List your Awards: Academic and Non-Academic Awards.** Pretend there are only five spaces; they don't mention a limit, but they don't want any attachments either.

You want to list at least 10 awards, using abbreviations and sometimes more than one item (if related) spaced together, so that you can fit as much as possible. Put your answers in columns (see below) or rows, so you can fit twice as many items. Below is what it should look like after you copy and paste.

High Honors/all Honors/AP classes	Captain Varsity Wrestling Tm — 2yrs
National Honors Society — 2yrs — Historian	Wrestling State Finalist, Regional
Biology Student of the Year	Champ/1 yr Reg. Finalist/1 yr & County Champ/2 yrs
Academic Team — 3 yrs	Student Government Rep — elected
Florida's Top 20 Scholars	Anchor Sweetheart — 2 yrs — elected
Varsity Football — 2 yrs/Super Knight	

OR the questions could go like this: **List all Academic Awards and Honors,** then **List all Extracurricular Activities:** There is no "Community Service" question, so you should include that under extracurricular activities. You should also incorporate non-academic awards under sports and club activities.

Academic Awards (also included is "Historian," because there is no separate question for non-academic awards or leadership positions and still needs to be listed somewhere):

Will graduate with High Honors, with all Honors/AP classes — 4 years

National Honors Society – 2 years – Historian
Biology Award – Student of the Year
Academic Team – 3 years
Florida's Top 20 Scholars

Extracurricular Activities (Remember, we are including non-academic awards as well as community service even though they weren't specified.):

VHS Football Team – 4 years
- Varsity – 2 years
- Super Knight Award – 2 years
- Summer Workouts – 4 years

VHS Wrestling Team – 2 years
- Varsity – 2 years
- Captain – 1 year
- State Finalist – 1 year
- Regional Champion – 1 year
- Semi–Finalist – 1 year
- Marion County Champion – 2 years

USA Wrestling Team – 2 years
VHS Baseball Team – 2 years
Student Government Representative (elected) – 4 years
Interact Service Club – 2 years
Anchor Service Club Sweetheart (elected) – 2 years
Vanguard High School Volunteer – 3 years – 110+ hours
- Assisted various office personnel with school start and ending

Anchor Service Club Sweetheart – 1.5 years – 4 hours monthly (not required)
- Help the homeless
- Assist with adopting a highway and clean up litter

Bible School Aide – 20 hours
Warm-up Ocala Campaign for the homeless and needy – 20 hours
Then this question may appear:

List all Leadership Skills or Examples:

This is where you put an officer position for a club, a captain of a team, a member of the varsity team of a sport, a member of the student government, or even a camp counselor or Sunday school teacher.

Example:

Leadership Skills

Historian of the National Honors Society *(an officer 'leads' the members)*
Varsity Football Team 2 years *(Varsity team 'leads' JV and freshman teams)*
Varsity Wrestling Team – 2 years
Captain – Wrestling Team *(Captain 'leads' the team by setting examples)*
Student Government Representative (elected) *(you are leading the school)*
Bible School Aide *(you are 'leading' children)*

There are so many different questions, yet they all result in using the same information. There is always a way to include everything, and it doesn't take that much time when you have all your data typed up and ready to use.

After answering all questions, move onto the essay, type it up, title it, and either copy it to the application, print as an attachment, or print, cut out with scissors, and tape to the application, then copy the entire page. You would be surprised how much time all of this saves. Now you can see how my daughter did seven different applications in about an hour and a half.

Chapter 7:
WRITING ESSAYS

Clarity, correct grammar, punctuation, and spelling should always be the essential foundations of an essay. I've read many essays with great content but misspelled words and horrible grammar. Not only have these been written by intelligent students but also by teachers. Not everyone is a writer. You may need some help organizing your thoughts and executing your topic properly. Never have someone write it for you but allow him or her to offer advice. Some of the strongest essays

I've read are from the student's heart and soul. You should always have someone proofread your work, if at all possible. You can ask an English teacher, a guidance counselor, a parent, or even a friend. Spell check works wonders, but it doesn't catch every minute error. You may accidently use the wrong word (even though it's spelled correctly) and it won't show up on spell check. I have also seen some rather strange words show up as okay through the program.

Read the directions carefully before you begin writing. Never go over the word limit or under the minimum either. Turning in an essay that is either too short or long can automatically disqualify you. Many applications ask for typed, double-spaced essays, and even stipulate a certain font or font size. There are even a few that want the essay handwritten in a certain ink color. If the directions aren't specific, remember that a simple font, typed, and double-spaced is always best. It's much easier for the judges to read your application if it's like this, especially if they have to read many essays. If you have to use your own handwriting, black ink is the easiest to read. Unless asked for, you can use print or cursive, whichever is neater.

You need to make sure you clearly understand the essay topic or question. The opening sentence should grab the attention of the reader, making him or her want to read more. Above all, don't get off topic. You need to follow the main idea throughout the entire essay. Start out with an introduction that shows the panelist that you understand the essay's topic and back up your essay with examples or explanations. Your personal experiences make the essay better. Whenever a student writes about overcoming obstacles, such as divorce, death, poverty, or even a type of disability, it displays strength and determination. Always finish with a strong conclusion that supports the main idea, something that can bring out a powerful emotion in the judges.

Always consider what the judges want. If you know that the judges are from the VFW, then you know that your audience esteems patriotism. If your judges are all females (such as an all women's club), don't sound too domineering or chauvinistic if you're male and show your strengths in being a young woman if you're female. If your essay is for an educational panel, then you should tie in the importance of education somewhere into your paper. Just as if the scholarship is from a certain business, you need to find out what type of business and use that to strengthen your essay. Your reviewers could be from an organization that is concerned with community service. Find out what your audience's concerns are and write about it, or if you cannot tie in that type of service, at least try to write about a similar kind of community service or experience. Don't go into religion or politics too deeply. There are so many different views on these controversial topics, and you don't want to insult someone's beliefs.

Fortunately, most scholarship essay questions are similar. The most popular question for seniors is, "What are your educational and career goals?" You need to research the type of education needed for your chosen career, the number of years of education needed,  and what you will financially need to get there. You also need to know what type of career opportunities your major will lead you to. Many students change their career goal before they complete their degree, but for now, write about the career you want at the moment. You also need to express why you've chosen your career choice. The main difference from application to application is the word requirement. Write an essay that is approximately 500 words ahead of time, so you can either cut or add parts depending on the particular word count. When shortening the length, keep the most important parts and even use contractions when possible. When lengthening it, write more about your dreams and desires, and if you still need more words, you can write either in more detail about one of your examples in the essay, or about an experience that led you to your career choice or even an interview with someone who works in that field.

Because most scholarships are only awarded once, most committees don't check up on you at college to see if you majored in the field you wrote about. You should be truthful and write about the major you intend to do. You can also write more passionately this way. Keep writing about the same major the entire year because many local scholarships have the same people on different scholarship committees.

Some of you might even change your mind about your career field during your senior year, but you need to focus on one career choice for local scholarships. A former student wanted to major in telecommunications with a possible backup career in nursing. For one application, she wrote about her desire to be in the telecommunications industry, and for another scholarship application, she wrote about nursing as a career. She won the first one from a local television company, and the second scholarship committee loved her essay on nursing, but there was a problem. One judge was on both scholarship committees. The judge called her and asked what was going on, and she explained about her double major. The committees allowed her to keep the first scholarship but could not award her the second. If she had written about wanting to have a double major on both applications, she would've had a better chance to win both because her essays were excellent. She eventually went into the law field, but the scholarship was for one year only, so it didn't matter that she switched her major.

This same situation also serves as another example but in a completely different way. This student had less than a 3.0 GPA with very few service hours, yet she was still the chosen winner for the scholarships because of the *content* of her essay. An essay can weigh the odds in your favor. I've seen countless students win a scholarship despite having a lower GPA or test scores versus other students because their essays were more substantial.

There are a very few applications that ask you to sign a paper declaring that you'll pay the organization back if you change your major, but I've only seen this once or twice. Some are also renewable for which you can reapply for each year. Other scholarships may even automatically renew if you keep up your GPA, but most want to see your college schedule to make sure that you're taking classes geared toward that major.

There are some local scholarship applications that will ask how you'll use your major to better your community. Even though most graduates don't plan to move back to their hometown, they should answer as if they'll return. Many panelists believe or hope that they're helping someone who will give back to their community one day. Think of how you could use your career to make your hometown a better place when writing your essay. Remember that there really is "no place like home" – you just do not realize it yet.

Another popular essay topic is community service and why it's important to the community or who it has impacted, including yourself. The main difference is the length of the essay. On most essays, the word requirement is about 500. You can cut down on time spent writing them by using the methods discussed above. On shorter essays, keep only the strongest points, and on the longer essays, explain why you did a certain type of community service and how it made a difference. This is a great time to use personal examples and relate how volunteering made a difference in someone's life, as well as your own.

Another common essay question is based on an event or a person who impacted your life, or even writing about an obstacle you've overcome. Always be honest, and be proud of any difficulty you've battled. At the moment, it may seem too personal to share, but panelists keep every essay confidential. Writing about any adversity shows what you've had to overcome and how nothing stopped you from accomplishing your dreams and goals in life. No matter what you write about, write with sincerity and pride about who you are and the direction you want to go in. Talk about your emotions or any learning experiences that helped you become the person you are today.

Keep a copy of all your essays, so you can simply edit and re-edit most of them in a short amount of time. You should also keep any well-written essays that you wrote for a class assignment because some scholarships may have an unusual essay question that you'll be able to answer using an old essay as reference. You might even be able to use some of your college essays or parts of them for scholarship applications.

Seniors always ask, *is there another essay to write?* And let out a huge sigh of despair because the rhetorical answer is yes. However, most senior essays are *not* a big deal. They are mostly opinion-based questions about being a student, and many can be used over and over again with only a few minor changes. Essays aren't worth stressing over. If you use your head and your heart, then you'll have no problem writing them. (But please double-check them!)

Chapter 8:
RECOMMENDATION LETTERS

Recommendation letters are extremely important for winning a scholarship. You always need to be prepared and have these letters ready because I've seen many students unable to turn in an application just because they didn't have their recommendation letters. Unfortunately, you have to depend on someone else to help you with this part. Many students put it off until the last minute, and the person may not have time to write one or it won't be the best letter he or she could've written due to a lack of time. When you ask someone for a  letter, always ask for it with plenty of notice. Two weeks is perfect, with a gentle reminder during the second week. A week ahead of time isn't that bad either, but two weeks is more courteous, and you might also receive a better letter of recommendation as well.

You should always choose the best person to write a reference letter. When you ask someone to write one for you, there are easy guidelines to remember. First, make sure you ask an adult who isn't related to you and who likes you. This may seem odd, but I've actually seen two students ask a teacher that they've had problems with for a letter of recommendation. Fortunately, I was able to read these letters and find a different reference for them. One letter wasn't nice, and the other was very basic and not personable; the reader wouldn't understand the writer's real opinion of the student. Never ask someone to write you a letter unless you know that they like and respect you. Teachers should be honest and professional when it comes to recommendation letters, but not everyone is that way. If they don't think a student deserves a good letter and he or she asks for one, they should either tell them that they don't have the time or they honestly cannot write the best letter for them. A teacher could also suggest another reference who is willing to write the letter. But not all adults act professionally. The best people to ask are the ones who have worked closely with you; therefore, they know you better than others and can usually write a more sincere letter.

Your recommendation letters also need to be well written. There are many people that may really like you but cannot formulate their thoughts. Some people just don't have the ability to give you a well-written letter. I've seen a letter consist of one short paragraph stating why the student is a very nice person and behaves well in class. This is why it's always better to receive more letters than you need, so you can pick the best ones to send.

You should always give the writer a copy of your résumé. He or she may know you in their classroom, or even through volunteering for an organization, but more than likely, they don't know all the different things you're involved in. Your résumé fills in the blanks for them and helps them write a better letter. It's also a good idea to sit down and talk with them if possible. Tell them more about yourself, and most importantly, let them know a few things about the scholarship application and what the committee is looking for. For instance, if it's a scholarship for pursuing an education major, talk about your desire to teach and any qualifications or dreams you have for that career.

Next, you need to make copies of your letters, if possible. Tell the writer that you are going to need more copies of the same letter for different scholarship applications, and ask them to save it to their computer. You can also provide a flash drive so he or she can save the letter onto it just in case a computer glitch occurs; and then you'll have a back-up copy. You still need to ask for a new letter for each scholarship so you can have an original signature and new date. An extra copy will help if the person is unavailable, and it can be reused, but only if it's also addressed in general (i.e. "Dear Scholarship Committee…"), so you can send the copied letter if you're unable to get a new letter. Some people like to personalize the letter, but if they will, have them address it to "Dear Scholarship Committee," so that the letter can be used for any application.

If possible (unless the letter is given to you in a sealed envelope), proofread the letter yourself. I've found incorrect information and misspelled names. We're all human, and we can all make mistakes, but try to correct them if you can.

Generally, you'll need at least two letters from two teachers (or your school's staff), one from an administrator (this includes your principal, assistant principal, and/or your guidance counselor), and one from someone else. Some scholarship applications want a letter from someone you did community service work for, and others just want a letter from someone outside your school. If you can get a letter from the person you volunteered for, you'll cover both of these bases. You can also ask an employer, your minister, or even a family doctor. If you can't get any of these, you can ask always your neighbors or even a family friend. Remember, these letters can also be used for college and job applications (with just a little bit of revision).

Make sure you always have them on hand because I've seen some local scholarships give the students a week to meet the deadline at the last second. Many students couldn't apply simply because they weren't prepared, didn't have any letters, or no one could write a letter for them on such short notice. This was a huge advantage for those students who were prepared. It doesn't hurt to ask people in the beginning of your senior year for a letter of recommendation for scholarships that you are applying for in the near future. Let them know that you are trying to get ahead of the game by giving them plenty of notice.

Always remember to sincerely thank the person who wrote the letter for you. When you've used the letter, it's a good idea to write them a short thank you note. Writing a good recommendation letter takes much time and thought. Sometimes, it's the recommendation letter that sways the scholarship panel's decision.

Chapter 9:
OWNING THE INTERVIEW

Some scholarship committees invite students to interviews to meet the semi-finalists. This interview could determine who the panelists will award the scholarship to. Be yourself as much as possible. First impressions are extremely important. Have confidence in yourself. Your application has succeeded this far, so there's nothing to stress about.

Dress in business attire. Guys should wear dress pants with a collared, buttoned-down shirt tucked in, as well as dress shoes. Avoid t-shirts and baggy pants. Ladies should wear a decent length dress, business skirt or dress pants with a classy top. Girls should avoid miniskirts and low-cut tops. Never wear jeans. You wouldn't believe the number of students who go to interviews in jeans, a T-shirt, and flip-flops. Avoid chewing gum as well. And, yes, I've seen actually seen adults chomp on gum during an interview, too.

When entering a room, stand tall, have a smile on your face, and look directly into the panelists' eyes. Shake each judge's hand firmly when you say hello and introduce yourself, starting with first and last name. Keep a positive attitude throughout the interview, as negativity can backfire onto their opinion of you.

Wait to be seated, and try not to cross your legs so your leg doesn't bounce. Never cross your arms or put your hands in your pockets during an interview because it seems disrespectful when you use bad body language. Sit up straight, and try not to fidget. Never look at a clock, your watch, or phone during an interview. Even though this seems ridiculous to point out, make sure your phone is turned off as well; in fact, it is best just to leave it in your car. Always make eye contact with the judge(s) during the interview and smile when you can while you answer questions.

When asked a question, pause shortly to think about your answer. Your answers should be brief, but don't limit them to a simple yes or no. When you take a short pause before answering, this shows that you're paying attention to the questions and didn't memorize your answers. At the same time, don't make your answers too lengthy. Talking too much can be obnoxious to the panelists. If you have an answer ready, just pause and silently repeat the question to yourself again. This may help you put your thoughts together in a better way. If you happen to stumble over an answer or have a nervous laugh, apologize, then repeat your answer. When the interview is over, as you leave, thank them for their time, and if appropriate, shake their hands again, and always wear a smile.

Before the Interview:

You'll need to look over your copy of the scholarship application beforehand, in case the panelists ask any questions that are on the original application. You should also reread your essay, if possible. This is another good time to look up the organization and see what they stand for. You never know when the extra knowledge will come in handy. One girl was actually asked what she knew about their club, and fortunately, she had read up on them and was prepared. She actually won the largest scholarship the committee awarded.

Here are some basic questions that are often asked during interviews. This will prepare you for your own interview. I've included a few suggestions on how to answer each question.

- **What are your career goals?** *Remember what you've written about in your career-goal essays.*

- **Why did you choose this career?** *Only you can answer this one, but think about it before you go so that your answer makes sense.*

- **Do you think you will make a difference with this career choice?** *Once again, you are the only one who can answer this question, but if all else fails, say something about helping people, helping the environment, or making a difference, which usually goes with most careers and how it may help your own community.*

- **What are your education goals?** *Once again, know how long it takes to get there, and what type of degree you need*

- **Where do you see yourself five years from now? Ten years from now?** *Be honest but brief. Five years from now, you may still be in school, or you might even be setting off to begin your career; and if that's the case, think about where you would like to work and what you would like to be doing there. Pick the best place possible. Ten years from now, try to be realistic because you'll be much more mature than you are now. You might have a family and be settled down. You can also think about advancement in your career path.*

- **How can you help your community after you begin your career?** *Act like you'll be coming back – you never know – and think about what you can do to help improve your community, wherever you are. You might be able to volunteer your time by relating it to whatever* *your career is or volunteering in other areas, just so it is something you would enjoy and can talk about with enthusiasm.*

- **Name someone who has had an impact on your life and tell us how he or she impacted it.** *This needs to be someone you admire. You can use a relative or even a "hero" whom you do not know but have always thought highly of, such as a person in history or someone more current. Have specific reasons why you look up to him or her. Someone may have done something to make you a better person, or could have also set such a wonderful example that you want to be like them, even if you don't know them.*

- **Tell us about an experience that impacted your life.** *If you have any obstacles that you have had to face, this is the time to talk about them. Not everyone has had obstacles in their lives, but perhaps you are thankful for what you have because of someone you know who has gone through hard times. If you cannot think of any, think about a time that you had to use teamwork, help others, or even an experience with an animal — just something that had a positive effect on you or others. It can be toward your grades, what type of person you want to be, or even something that helped you make a decision about your career choice. It can even be about something that you had to deal with in regards to your peers or your family.*

- **What is your best quality? What is your worse quality?** *Think about these questions to help you: What do your friends like about you? What would your parents or teachers say? What do you like about yourself? As far as the worse quality — what is there that you would like to change?*

- **If you could change one thing in education, your community, the world, or your life, what would it be and how would you change it?** *Make sure that this is a realistic solution. It doesn't have to be something major, like save the world or have world peace, but* *something you can answer with passion, something that you really care about. It can be as simple as wanting to help the needy or the environment, which you can do by volunteering. It only takes one person to get something started.*

- **Why should you be a recipient of this scholarship?** *This is where you can tell how hard you've worked to be where you are today – your grades, your community service, your sport, your club. Don't say, "I should be the recipient"; instead, say something like, "I would be honored to be the recipient of your scholarship because I have…" It could even be because of your desire to further your education or pursue your dream career.*

- **Why do you need this scholarship?** *You will be able to say that, without help, it would be difficult to attend college, or you could even say that you want to pay for education yourself and be independent from your parents, or that your family has financial problems and that this scholarship would help you so much with your future. If you come from a middle class family, you can tell them that your parents make too much money to receive financial assistance but don't make enough to help pay for college. Also, if your degree requires five or eight years of schooling, it doesn't matter what your parents make – that would be a very expensive education for anyone.*

- **What is the most important quality you look for in a friend?** *Be honest; this is an easy question. Just make sure it is something you admire or strive to be as well.*

- **Describe yourself in one word.** *Make it positive! It could be reliable, humorous, caring, loving, outgoing, responsible, trustworthy, friendly, loyal, dependable, or witty. There are so many positive words. Think about this question ahead of time. But be ready for a reason if they ask for an example.*

All these questions have been asked at one point or another during scholarship interviews. They are all a little different, but if you think about these questions ahead of time, you'll be prepared to go into the interview with confidence. No one can give you any set questions or answers. These are only suggestions to get you to use your imagination. Just remember to be positive at all times and think back to your résumé. If you go over the sample questions with another adult, have him or her ask questions and listen to your answers. Then they can critique your responses to help you out. Go to more than one person if you aren't satisfied with their reactions or help.

Going to an interview will be a fantastic experience for you even if you don't win. Throughout life, you'll go to college interviews, job interviews and even perhaps host your own in the future. Interviews pave the way for you throughout your career and life.

Chapter 10:
FAFSA AND STATE GRANTS

The Free Application for Federal Student Aid (FAFSA) is a federally funded, nationwide program, even though each state has its own type of state grants, scholarships, and loans. The FAFSA has its own rules for grants and loans, which are based on financial need. I've learned some useful information about this program that may benefit you, no matter what state you live in.

FAFSA is a financial-need application that must be renewed annually, no matter what your income is. It's based on your parents' income and yours (if you filed taxes) from the previous year. Besides the amount of your adjusted gross income, FAFSA takes into consideration the number of people living in your household and immediate family members (also in your household) attending college. They don't take into consideration the normal bills (rent/mortgage, utilities, phone, gas, etc.) everyone has to pay.

The Student Aid Report (SAR) from the FAFSA is sent to you, as well your college choices, and then the financial aid office determines the amount you'll receive, and whether it will be a grant (which you don't pay back) or a low-interest rate loan. There are two different types of student loans: subsidized loans, in which interest starts after graduation, or unsubsidized loans, where the interest is paid while you are in college. If your loan need is greater than what they will lend a student, there are also parent plus loans, where the parent pays a monthly fee upon receiving the loan. All of these loans do have certain requirements, such as the amount and your credit. But as this is a book on scholarships and ways to avoid loans, so you can go to either your college's financial aid department or online to www.FAFSA.ed.gov for more information on loan conditions.

If you've had a change that's affected the upcoming school year versus the previous year, the financial aid office will usually work with you and readjust your amount of grants or loans you receive. For example, you'll be attending college in Fall 2015, and the application is filled out with 2014 tax forms. If your income for 2015 drops by a good amount, perhaps because of job loss, divorce, a death in the family, a huge hospital bill, or new financial care for an elderly relative, then you should contact the college's financial aid office and let them know. They may ask for something in writing, such as a notarized paper, or even a paycheck stub, but they'll generally help you out. It never hurts to ask.

A student must use his or her parents' income for the FAFSA if he or she depends on them. There are a few cases where a student is independent, however, it's difficult to verify this. If a parent refuses to help pay for his or her child's college expenses or tells him or her to move out, the student still has to list their parent's income until age 25. If the student gets married or is in the armed forces before 25, then they will be declared independent. Students can also be independent if they are pregnant or have a child, but they have to prove that they pay for over 50 percent of the baby's expenses. Students can also become emancipated, but it takes time, work, and has to be accepted by the courts as well.

There are some other circumstances where students can declare themselves as independent. For example, if the student is a ward of the court or foster child, they're considered independent. With the amount of homeless people growing over the past few years, students can declare themselves "homeless" (their family may live with another family, in a hotel or at a homeless shelter) and are considered independent from then on. If the high school is aware of situations like this, then declaring independence is much easier if you can get the school to make it official on the student's transcripts.

In one young man's circumstances, his father kicked him out and refused to give him any income information for FAFSA. This wasn't a situation where the father and son just had a disagreement; the father just didn't care and had mental- and drug-related problems. Even though he was living with his coach and family because he had nowhere to go, the financial aid office at one university made him use his mother's income, even though she lived in another state and didn't support him; he had only talked to her twice in the past four years. This turned him into a non-resident of the state where he lived because they were using income from an out-of-state parent, and his tuition fees more than tripled. Luckily, another college, with the help of letters from instructors at his high school (and the coach he lived with), made it possible for him to be able to file as independent, and he was awarded grants from the FAFSA that helped him pay his way through college.

Another young man's mother passed away, and his biological father wasn't in his life. I talked to the financial aid office, and even though his transcripts declared him as homeless, they also asked for teachers and coaches to write a letter verifying his situation; only then would they declare him independent. Every college is different, just as each circumstance is. There was a young girl who lived with another family, and she paid them rent and helped with other bills. She didn't have support from anyone, so when we called the financial aid office, they claimed her as independent without any letters needed to verify this.

Not every college will do that, but if a student is having trouble receiving financial aid and he or she really needs it, then perhaps the student should try to find a college that will work with him or her. Remember, there are only a few ways that determine your independent status under 25, so visit the FAFSA website for more information on what your status will be.

There is also a work-study program through FAFSA. The program involves working in one of the college's departments. Although it's available at many colleges, it isn't offered at all of them. The financial aid department in each college decides the amount of work-study awards the college will provide and who can receive them. This amount is determined by financial need, but priority doesn't necessarily go to those who are the most financially needy. On the FAFSA application, it's a good idea to answer 'yes' to the work-study program, even if the student might not qualify or if they do not plan to work while in college. If you mark 'no' to the question, you won't be able to apply to any job at the college. You never know what job may come up or what event may happen in your life where you might need to go to work. Your college doesn't require you to work there even if you do answer yes. The positive side of the work-study program is that they pay more than minimum wage, sometimes even allowing students to complete homework while they are on the clock and enable them to have a job that is in the department of their own major.

The Pell and FSEOG grants are given to those with financial need. The FSEOG is specifically for those with significant financial need. Many parents cannot afford to send their children away to college, and if your income is considered middle class or above, you *may* qualify for loans, but most likely not for grants. If you're closer to a low middle class status, you may be eligible for a small portion of a Pell grant. The grants are mainly for low-income families.

Some colleges also have additional financial need or academic financial need grants as well, but there can be on glitch in this system. If your bills are paid (including room and board), and the student receives a scholarship that exceeds that amount, most colleges won't give additional money to that student. One student received scholarships and grants that gave her a full ride to college. When she won another $3,000 scholarship a month later, the financial aid department kept the money and told her that it went into one of the grants they had given her. This only can happen if all bills have been paid: tuition and fees, books, and room and board.

Filling out a FAFSA application also shows scholarship panels or colleges that you have tried to receive help through federal aid. This could be a determining factor in regards to winning a scholarship. If they see that you haven't received any federal help, hopefully, they'll understand that you need extra help to afford college. I actually convinced a local scholarship panel that was based on financial need to change their requirements to financial need with certain circumstances. They looked into students whose parents had middle-class incomes and the type of the degree the student was pursuing and opened up their scholarship to a wider range of applicants. One of our local community colleges gave out some scholarships for students whose parents did not qualify for financial need grants, and did not make enough to fund their child's education, but only after they filled out the FAFSA first.

An important fact to remember on grants is that if you drop a class before the 60 percent mark in a semester, then you'll owe the college and/or the Department of Education money then you will have to pay back the money you received from the grant. Once you owe them money, it will jeopardize your future eligibility status for financial aid, including loans until it is paid back. Check with your school on their rules for maintaining your financial aid because each school has its own criteria.

Something else to remember is that grants don't last forever. If you plan on going to graduate school and have received a bachelor's degree already, you may still be eligible for federal loans, but no longer federal grants. Unfortunately, they end once your bachelor's degree is obtained.

You need to fill out the Federal Application for Free Student Aid form as soon as possible, especially if you're eligible for financial need. You cannot apply until January of the year you will be attending college in the fall. Once again, you need to reapply every year. Each

school gets so much money from the government, and you need to try and get it before they hand it all out. One financial aid officer told me that the first applications receive larger amounts of money than the late ones. If you're attending college in the summer before July 1 of any year, then you need to fill out a FAFSA form from the previous year, the 2013-2014 application using your 2012 income. Then if you attend in either summer after July 1 or in the fall of 2014, you would apply (or reapply), with the FAFSA 2014-2015, using your 2013 income. Yes, it gets confusing, but refer to **www.FAFSA.ed.gov** for more information.

Financial aid offices should have the FAFSA application for you. But if you do it online, you'll receive your results much faster. Staff members can also help you fill out paperwork if needed. You need to be careful when you apply online, and make sure you're on the correct website. When you google FAFSA, the first website is FAFSA.com. Students have come to me and asked if they have to pay the $89 fee on this website. Don't pay anything—FAFSA is FREE, and the first two letters, FA, in FAFSA stand for "free application". Just make sure that you go to **www.FAFSA.ed.gov**. I've been told the other website isn't illegal and will still send in your information as a third party, but it sounds pretty illegal to me. Who in their right mind wants to pay for a free application?

State grants, though, are a different story. Scholarship awards don't usually affect state grants because they aren't based on financial need. State grants vary from state to state and can change from year to year if funding is low. They work much differently from federal grants. There may be a few based on financial need, but they are mostly based on different qualifications. My daughter received a grant for education majors, called The Chappie James grant, which sadly, is no longer in effect. The grant was sent to her college, and in return, they reimbursed her anything that went over her tuition. The money was used for books and then put into a special college savings account for future college needs. This grant wasn't based on income at all.

Florida also has several other state grants, but not as many as there used to be. Last year, they had to fill out the FAFSA form to be eligible for state grants in Florida, no matter what they are based on (one more reason to fill it out), but this is also something that can change from year to year. Florida students automatically apply for state grants when they apply for the Florida Bright Future Scholarships. This is a wonderful program that used to pay between 75 and 100 percent of tuition at Florida public colleges. Now it's much less, averaging around 40 percent of tuition because of the economy. It's based on classes taken during high school, a student's GPA, and ACT or SAT scores, and not financial need.

If you live in Florida, parents and students need to visit a guidance counselor to see if they qualify or what they need to do to be eligible. You can also go online to **www.floridastudentfinancialaid.org** for more information. This scholarship is guaranteed as long as you meet the criteria, and there are three different ways you can do that. If you qualify for Florida Bright Futures, or even think you will, apply online early (usually starting in December). It automatically makes you eligible for other state grants, too.

Students have to maintain a certain GPA during college for it to continue. This can also be used for private colleges or vocational schools in Florida, but students only receive the public college's tuition amount. This amount can also change at any time, and it has in the past. If the allotted amount decreases, this can affect students already in college, as well as incoming freshmen.

The Florida Bright Futures Scholarships is a fantastic program, and I could probably write an entire chapter on it. But if you are outside of Florida, I urge you to talk to your guidance counselor to see what scholarships and grants you may be eligible for. If the counselor's advice is vague, call the state financial aid office (usually a toll-free number). No matter what state you live in, find out about your state's grants and any other special programs, like the Florida Bright Futures. I've provided every state's financial aid office information at the end of the book. Also, be sure to ask your college's financial aid office if they have any programs for in state residents.

Loans should be used as a last resort only. Depending on your family's income, you can be awarded a subsidized and an unsubsidized loan at the same time. This would be a total of four different loans for one year. Each count as a separate loan per semester, too. If you had both types of loans each year, you could end up with 16 different loans after graduation. Unless you are able to consolidate them all into one loan, it will hurt your credit to have so many loans. Keep your loans to the minimum because I've known people who were still paying off their school loans 10 to 15 years after graduation. One of my friends, was almost unable to purchase a house because of her student loans. Another student owes $40,000, pays $400-$500 monthly and can barely live on her own. Many students believe they'll make so much money after they graduate and will be able pay off these debts easily, but this isn't always true. Each career has starting positions that may start off with an initial income that is low, and it may take them several years to earn their dream salary—and loan payments aren't put on hold until you're rich.

Be careful how you use loans when you receive them. Many students use loan money for things beyond college expenses, such as trips or unnecessary luxuries. However, they will realize their mistake when payments come around.

When your college sends you a financial aid report, check for any schol-arships, grants, or loans that you are eligible for. Many colleges title this "Financial Aid Awards". Loans and work-study programs are included on this page. Loans are not awards because you have to pay them back, and the work-study's money is not yours until you actually have the job and work. So take that into account when figuring out your budget.

Everyone needs to apply for the FAFSA. Remember, it's not a complicated process; you just need to follow the directions carefully. Many people assume that they make too much money to qualify even for loans, but this isn't always true. If you need them, these loans have low interest rates and much more flexible repayment options than private loans. You just need to remember that FAFSA is there to help students, but unfortunately, not all students benefit from it. But until you apply, you will never know if it could assist you.

Chapter 11:
HOW DO I RECEIVE SCHOLARSHIP AWARDS?

Once you've won a scholarship, how do you actually receive it? And what if you aren't sure what college you'll attend when you find out you won a scholarship? Well, it depends on the committee and how it disburses the scholarship.

Don't worry about your college choice at this time, because most scholarships want you to see your proof of acceptance before disbursing the money. Some scholarship applications may even ask for proof of acceptance when you first apply. If you have proof of one college or more, go ahead and send it, but add a note telling the panelists that you haven't made your decision yet and why. This could be because you're still waiting to hear from your first choice or you want to see which college will award you the most money. If you're still undecided by the end of the school year and have won a scholarship, simply call or write the "scholarship donor" and tell

them you're still making your final decision but will let them know your choice as soon as possible.

Most scholarships are sent directly to the college's financial aid office. Usually, the money arrives there before you even schedule your classes, so it's there for your use when paying fees and tuition. Some scholarships are sent to your home address, but the check is made out to the college. It's your responsibility to send it to the financial aid office as soon as you can. Before you mail it, call and see where the check should be sent, and then call again to make sure they received it. Then, there are the easiest scholarships to take care of; those are scholarships that are sent to you, and the check is made out in your name. If this is the case, I strongly urge you to put the money in a separate savings account, to be used just for college expenses.

Here are some examples of how it's generally done. Let's say you have received a scholarship for $2,000, and it was sent directly to your college. You sign up for classes, and it costs $2,000 for one semester. In your mind, you might believe that the cost is fully covered. But many colleges take the award money and divide the amount into two semesters, giving you $1,000 of the $2,000 scholarship for the first semester, and the second half for the second semester; so you still owe $1,000 for the first semester. However, if your scholarship amount is more than tuition and fees, the school may do one of several things; they might apply it to your dormitory account, put it on a college credit card, or send you a check for the leftover amount. Deposit any leftover college money into your own private savings account, even if it is on the credit card they gave you so that you will have sole control over it.

There are scholarships that award you savings bonds, but that happens less and less because there is more paperwork to fill out and more rules to follow for the donor. Savings bonds don't get sent to your college because they're most likely made out in your name. If you do receive one, see how long it takes to mature into the full amount. One savings bond that was given out to my students didn't mature until 30 years later. You have the choice of either cashing it in before that allotted time but you lose a significant amount of money. But 30 years is a long time to hang on to something, so if you want, you can turn in it before its maturity; the bond will usually refund you half the amount of the savings bond normally after one year's wait. Even that's better than nothing, and that money will come in handy a year later.

One of the most important things to remember is making sure you know exactly how much money you have coming to you. Keep a record of all awards and even loans, just to make sure you receive all your money. Colleges can make mistakes because the human factor comes into play. It would be a good idea to also make a copy of any checks sent to you before you deposit them, so you can prove what was sent to you.

When my daughter won several different scholarships, one of the first ones was for $1,000 for the college of her choice. The committee divided it up into two semesters. When I asked what would happen to the second half of the scholarship if she switched colleges in the spring semester, the committee said it would send the remainder back to the donor. If she did change colleges, she would have to call the scholarship committee and ask them to resend the $500 to another college. This is a hassle, but what can you do? You need to make sure that you follow up on this money, too. If the scholarship is directly from your college, then it's only for that particular college and leaving forfeits the scholarship. Generally, the majority of colleges divide the scholarship into two semesters because that's how any grants or loans from FAFSA are given out.

Now, let's say you were awarded $7,000 total, and your bill for one semester is $3,000 (which depends on the amount each college charges and how many credit hours you're taking). If it's a college that doesn't divide the amount into two semesters, they would send you a refund of $4,000, but if they divide it into two semesters ($3,500 towards the $3,000 tuition), the refund for the first semester would be for $500. After paying for your second term, you should then receive the remainder (in this case, another $500 if the tuition is the same) of the amount that goes over tuition.

At most colleges, you cannot use money in your college account to pay for books until it's sent to you. The bookstore is usually a separate entity from the college, and because the refund usually takes a few weeks to get there, you'll have to pay for your books up front and reimburse yourself when you receive the scholarship refund. Because you can get better prices for books online, the money would have to come directly from you anyways when you buy a book from a website.

You need to keep track of *all* scholarships, grants, and loans that you are awarded. I can't stress this enough. Like I said, mistakes happen. During my daughter's first year at college, she had more than enough scholarships to pay for her classes. Even though her college divided up her scholarship money into two semesters, they still owed her quite a bit just from the first semester.

In Florida, where we have the Florida Bright Futures, she was awarded the Florida Bright Futures Medallion, which covered 75 percent of her tuition at the time. This money is sent to the student's college, but some colleges don't always apply it toward the students' fees upon registration for the first semester. He or she has to pay up front for their first semester, and then the college will send them a check from the Bright Futures, but not until after the add/drop period. Jessica's first semester was already paid for by other scholarships, and  so she still had over $1,000 extra. After receiving the check, she didn't pay attention to the fact that she hadn't received her Bright Futures money.

However, I kept track of all her scholarships, how much was spent, and how much she was reimbursed. When the add/drop period was over (and several students I knew already received their Bright Futures money), I called the financial aid office. They told me that my daughter never returned the letter to the state program notifying them which college she attended. Then I called the state financial aid office in Tallahassee and told them what the college had told me. They told me that they had received the letter from Jessica naming her college and the money was already sent to the college in her name. Afterward, I went directly to the senior guidance counselor, who called the college and told them that they had exactly one week to get the check in the mail to Jessica or she would contact a lawyer. And the money was there in less than a week. Sometimes, students' money seems to fall through the cracks, and sadly enough, if someone isn't paying attention, it will never appear.

Four years after correcting Jessica's problems, my son started college, and problems started midway through his first semester. Michael also received Bright Futures, along with other scholarships, too. Some checks were sent directly to him (after he had sent them proof of enrollment) and some to the college, so keeping track of his money was a little confusing. About two months into the first semester, his college sent him notice that some additional scholarships had been awarded to him through their financial aid office; he was sent four different letters, two separate letters for each of two different scholarships. The first set was $200 for the fall and a second letter from the same scholarship for $200 for the spring semester. The second set of letters was from another scholarship for $300 for fall and another $300 for spring. He had already paid in full and even received reimbursement for the fall semester, so he should have had a $500 check sent to him in the mail. Instead, they sent him a check for $206, an odd number that didn't quite make sense.

Two months passed, and he still didn't receive anything else, so we called the financial aid department. We were told that he had a balance of $294 for the fall semester, but they had just never sent it. We were then told that he should receive a check in the mail within the next two weeks. Four weeks later we called again, and we were told that he would receive a check within a week. He finally got a check, but it was only for $10 (and for a different reason). Again, none of this answered our questions and did not have anything to do with his scholarship money.

Finally, after many inquiries from us to their office, we were told that they only had a copy of two letters from their own financial aid department to Michael. We had to tell them that we had four letters, and we would bring them in or fax the letters to them. They suddenly found all of his scholarship letters and money and finally sent the remainder of the money to him. But the problems didn't stop there.

I had carefully calculated what his fees and tuition ended up costing, how much scholarship money he had, and what they had reimbursed him. I was relieved when the check they sent for his second semester was the correct amount (except for the Bright Futures), which included the money they had owed him from their own scholarships they had awarded him. I kept a close eye on the dates when the Bright Futures money was supposed to come out for the second semester. I gave them six weeks, and once again, called the financial aid office because it never came. They told me that they automatically apply Bright Futures when students enroll for their second semester and that a check had already been sent. He had received a check, but the amount didn't include the Bright Futures money; it was only for the scholarship money that had been in his account previously. The office looked at his records and said he was paid in full. I then went over everything with them; the correct amount of each scholarship, tuition and fees, the reimbursement checks that he had received from them, and the amount that they still owed him. I had to do this twice, even asking her to write it down the third time, and then she finally told me that she would turn this over to her supervisor. The next day, my son finally received the correct amount that they owed him.

There are so many students out there who don't receive the full amount of money they deserve. My own children just assumed that their college had paid them correctly, because tuition and other fees were fully paid, and they each received a nice amount to deposit for other expenses. Needless to say, I was pretty upset that I had to call and demand a refund for the correct amount of money for both of my children. I even called the same counselor who helped me with Jessica and told her about Michael's injustice. She wanted me to write everything down and give it to the dean's wife, because she worked at our school. I did this, but there was little they could do to sort this out. I felt that it was my duty to do this on behalf of other students and their parents, so I always tell students to keep a close eye on their money. You have to pay attention to every dollar that should come your way. Many students and parents don't realize exactly how to do this or that there is a need for double-checking the amount. It's not that difficult, as long as you keep tabs on what has been won from scholarships or received through grants or loans, how much has been paid for tuition and fees, and then the amount that needs to be reimbursed.

Carefully watch over the money sent to you from loans, as well. If the college says the office sent you a check for $2,000 and you only received $1,000, the only real way to prove this is a copy of the check before you deposited or cashed it. The same goes for scholarship reimbursements. Keep a copy of the check. Sadly, you never know when you may have to prove what was sent to you.

I just came across another problem this year with one senior from the previous year. He filled out the FAFSA form and answered yes to the question about needing loans just in case he might need them (which is usually a good way to answer the question). He got more than enough money from scholarships and didn't need any loans. He never filled out any more forms, which most colleges require you to do when you receive loans, so that you can choose your lender and agree to pay them back. One day, he checked his account and saw that he had over $900 in loans for him for each semester, even though he never filled out the loan forms. He called and was told that money was there for him just in case, but it showed up as a loan.

He was able to remove the loan because he never borrowed any money, but what would've happened if he hadn't checked his account? The financial office told him that the loan might have shown up by the time he grad-uated and that he would have to pay it back if he didn't have any proof of not touching the loan. So keep track of your money. Another case was where a student applied for a private loan and received more than she needed. This girl had been eligible for the Pell Grant the previous year, but the second year she applied she was denied the grant. Her parents' income had not changed, so she called FAFSA directly. After several phone calls, she found out that the private loan somehow showed up as money in her savings account, and that was why they had denied her the grants. So please be very careful before accepting any private loans. Check with your college's financial aid department and check with FAFSA, if in doubt.

There are other things to look out for, too. Some scholarships specify when committees will send money. If this is the case, make sure you call the financial aid office before tuition is due, so you won't have to pay out of your own pocket. Always make sure you've sent the scholarship committee your college information and proof of enrollment whether it's required or not. Even if the organization hasn't given you a timeline for when the scholarship money will come, you still need to send them your proof of enrollment and wait three to four weeks before you can call the college's financial aid office to see if they've received the money yet. If they haven't, wait another week or two and call again. If your college still hasn't received the money, you may have to call the scholarship committee yourself to find out when the money will arrive there. Be polite, even if you're frustrated.

A local club once gave out scholarships, and between sending the award letter and the money, the money never got sent until the winner reminded them. It turned out that there was a newly elected officer who didn't know about it. Another student didn't know what happened to one of her scholarships. Apparently, the committee had lost her address and was glad I had contacted them about her scholarship. So keep a copy of all confirmation letters, just as you've kept a copy of all applications. You never know when you may need it for proof or to contact someone about an issue.

When you receive a scholarship, a thank-you note is a must. You can either send it right away or after you've received your scholarship money, but please don't forget to send a letter. It's the least you can do when someone's been generous enough to help you finance your education. You never know if a scholarship (especially local ones) may renew itself, and that thank you letter just might keep your name in someone's mind.

Chapter 12:
STAY SCAM-FREE

Scholarship scams come in many forms. There are so many free scholarship searches (see the last page of this chapter for websites), and you can always go to the public library and use scholarship books to search for even more. You should never have to pay for a search; you apply for scholarships to win money, not dish it out in hopes of winning. I've seen searches that charge between $40 and $50 for their services and actually do search for scholarships. Most scholarships were national-based, some no longer existed and there were no local ones. I compared my own list of scholarships to theirs; I had over 85 percent of them, and it didn't cost me anything, except time, to compile my list.

Be wary of scholarship applications that request money to apply. However, there are exceptions. Contests sometimes ask for an entry fee, and most of these are artistic-based. Many are legit; just don't spend too much money on them. I've seen some basic, non-artistic applications ask for as much as $20. Don't waste your money.

One of the worst scams is receiving an official-looking letter on a fancy letterhead, which invites you to participate in a scholarship (or college) information workshop or presentation. These meetings are usually held in a conference room at a reputable hotel or even the public library. The speakers talk about helping you apply to colleges and for scholarships, making the entire process easier. They promise that you'll win a scholarship and your chances of getting into a difficult college will be much higher with their help.

First of all, you don't need to pay anyone to help you with college applications. There is already a college application fee you have to pay, so don't spend any more money than you need to. Ask your guidance counselor for help with applications. You can also go to an English teacher if you need help with writing essays, if one is required, or you can search for examples of college essays online.

There's another catch to their scheme: *Pay us now, and we guarantee you'll receive a scholarship.* No one can promise that. There was a company that came to my town, and one young man and his mother paid $1,000 for them to help him with scholarships. They guaranteed that he would receive at least $2,000 minimum. The first document he received from this company was a preview of what he could get from the Free Application for Federal Student Aid (FAFSA).

The FAFSA form is just that – a free application. This young man's mother lived on a very low income, and the only way she was able to pay for this "help" was from a small inheritance. Anyone could've predicted that he would receive grants from federal aid because of his mother's income. Another month or two went by, and he received a nice package from this company. It was in a binder, and each page was in plastic sheet protectors. What the holders contained, though, was a joke. They had simply laid out everything he should receive from FAFSA in grants and student loans, just in more detail. They hadn't sent him one scholarship application.

I called the company and told them that what they sent was a waste because the young man's college was sending the same information for free, just not in such nice wrapping as theirs. I then asked them about scholarship applications, and they only talked about what they had done for him—which was nothing. I got an attorney for the young man, but unfortunately, he never told me what happened afterward, so I assume he was unable to get any money back. I never saw the copy of the signed contract, so I always wondered if the fine print said something about guaranteeing money but not where it would come from. Even I could've guaranteed that he would receive money from the government. But no one is ever guaranteed about winning a scholarship.

It's just a shame that I had all these applications that he could've applied for, and they wouldn't have cost him anything besides his time. His mother wasted her inheritance and could've used it toward paying for his education instead. If someone does write a check to one of these scams, there is sometimes a two- or three-day time frame where they can null the check. This actually worked for a parent that came to my workshop (which, by the way, is free). She wrote out a check the previous day to one of these companies and was happily able to get her money back. However, there are too many other people who fall for these scams and lose their money on them.

My students receive these letters every year, asking them to attend a workshop, and always under a new company title. Some of them will offer a 'free' workshop. The workshop is free, but the meeting they setup afterward will not be. Parents and students ask for my advice about whether or not they should go. I tell them what I have just told you, and to attend if they want to but never pay money for anything. Most parents throw the letters away, but there are always a few that decide to attend, hoping they can receive free money, but find out that the price is steep. Each time the scammers come to my town, they come under a different name and usually rent out different places. One even had their meeting at a popular public university. The letter made it sound like they were part of the college, but didn't come right out and say it. There wasn't a college logo on the letterhead either. I contacted the college and was told that whoever this company was, they were not affiliated with their college and that they were only renting a room from them. These scam companies always seem to rent a room at reputable places, which makes them seem trustworthy.

Just remember: NEVER pay for what you can get for free.

Here are phrases to watch out for (and my responses):

- "We can guarantee you financial aid, or you will get your money back." *Are they talking about loans by any chance? Anyone can apply to FAFSA or go to the bank for those.*
- "You can't get this information anywhere else or from anyone else." *Except at school from your counselor or by surfing the Internet.*
- "You must have a credit card, bank account number, or social security number in order to apply for this scholarship." *I have yet to see ANY scholarship application that requires any of these.*
- "We'll do all of the work for you." *Something for nothing? No one but you can do this.*
- "This scholarship will cost you some money." *Maybe on Wall Street, but not for scholarships.*
- "You are a semi-finalist (or finalist), or you have been selected (and you never even applied)." *When it seems too good to be true, it usually is.*

So please don't pay anyone to help you win a scholarship. Do the work yourself and save the money for a better purpose. It all goes back to what my father used to tell me: "You do not get something for nothing; life just is not that easy."

A Few Scholarship Websites to Try:

- **www.scholarships.com**
- **www.fastweb.com**
- **www.student.gov**

- www.finaid.org/scholarships
- www.fastaid.com
- www.collegenet.com
- www.finaid.org
- www.collegeanswer.com
- www.collegeboard.org
- www.princetonreview.com/sallie-mae-scholarship.aspx
- www.cappex.com/scholarships/
- www.scholarshipexperts.com
- www.scholarships.collegetoolkit.com
- www.collegeprowler.com
- www.kaarme.com
- www.collegeapps.about.com

Chapter 13:

OTHER TIPS ON SAVING MONEY

There are a few other ways to fund your college education besides scholarships and loans. You may be able to find a business that will repay all or at least part of your loans if you work for them for a certain length of time after you receive your degree. This could be through a local hospital, auto shop, or pharmacy, just to name a few. The Central Intelligence Agency (CIA), Defense Intelligence Agency, and National Security Agency all have scholarships that pay tuition, room and board, and books stipends as well as a summer job with pay. You have to work a year and a half for every year you receive the scholarship, but if that is where you want to pursue a career, then this is a great way to get your foot in the door and have school paid for as well.

Some businesses have college tuition reimbursement programs for their employees, such as Lockheed Martin, Home Depot, Apple, Walgreens, and Publix, and of course you will still have to maintain a career with them for a specified amount of time to make their investment in you worthwhile.

You will need to check with their corporate offices to see if they still offer these opportunities. There are also nursing and teaching programs (i.e. Teach For America) that pay for college if you work in a low-income area.

Additional websites for reimbursement (for specific majors):

www.studentaid.ed.gov
www.hrsa.gov/index.html

You can also intern during the summer. Many majors require you to do an internship, and some businesses even pay you. This could also lead to a full-time career if they like you and could possibly pay for your tuition.

Buy your books from the least expensive place. Go online and do a comparison search. They're almost always cheaper than the bookstore. Buy used books when you can and resell the ones you don't want to keep.

Live at home. I know that many students just *have* to leave home, but if you can stay there, you'll save $8,000 to $10,000 annually. The cost of living is usually higher than tuition and fees. And if you work, you'll rarely see your family between school, work, and studying. Or you could always find a roommate to help cut down the cost of living on your own.

College dorms are usually more expensive then renting an apartment, but many colleges have nearby apartments that are rented out to college students. If you live in a quad with four bedrooms and two or four bathrooms, you only have to share the kitchen and living room, have a bedroom all to yourself, and either have your own bathroom or only have to share with one other person instead of the entire floor of a dorm and for all of this you will pay less than living in a dorm.

Lastly, attend an affordable college. Public in-state colleges are the least expensive, with community colleges costing even less. If you go to college out of state, your rates could triple. Some colleges allow out of state students to claim residency after the first year, or might even waive the non-resident tuition, but you need to contact the financial aid department to find out. Private schools are extremely costly and love to offer huge scholarships that, in reality, only relieve a small percentage of the cost. They will also 'award' you a wonderful financial aid packet that includes huge loans—loans that will double by the time you pay them off.

As time passes, more and more Ivy League schools do not want the students to have loans and will help finance most of your education if you get accepted and have financial need. If you don't have financial need, they'll make you pay the 'expected family contribution' (determined by FAFSA), but that amount doesn't cover other bills that your parents have to pay.

You need to look at the total costs of where you decide to go. Yes, most kids want to go to top-ranked schools, but many careers are actually found through internships, not the school they attended. If you're eventually going to get a master's degree or doctorate, and you really feel that you have to attend a particular expensive school for that major, then you can always transfer to the higher ranked school for those higher degrees, and receive your bachelor's degree at a lesser cost.

Chapter 14:
CONCLUSION

There are a variety of ways to find scholarship information and applications for students. My method, I'm sure, is one of many.

I start with the all the local scholarships that come into the guidance office or go directly to the senior guidance counselor. Many counselors at other schools simply file these and hold them for students to go through on their own time. I retrieve them, advertise them, make copies, and then file them. I also send out over 100 letters of request for applications every year. This happens less each year because many applications are now online. So I simply search for those online instead of mailing them requests. Make sure that you type in the year of the application you are looking for, because you can spend too much time searching and finding all of the previous year's scholarship applications first, rather than going straight to the current year's application.

I keep a list of previous scholarships and search for them about two or three months before they are due. The website will usually tell me to return at a later date. I have folders of each month for these, so I can remember to check them on time. I still go on scholarship searches because there are always new applications for specific students and majors.

Remember that even though these students are seniors, they still need extra guidance to help them transition to college. I try to make it easier for them by reading every scholarship application I receive, typing a bulletin stating only the basics (i.e. requirements, eligibility, attachments and essays needed, amount of scholarship, and deadlines) and simplifying the whole process for them. If it's an online application, I print out as much information as possible, just so students have extra help. Now that so many applications are completed online, I finally created a method to differentiate between online and hardcopy scholarships by highlighting each one accordingly. Whether it's an online or hardcopy, I type them up into my bulletin using the same method. I start out with the title (which is what they are filed under in my scholarship files), with the grade level next. I also code the different grade levels with colored check marks on the left side of the description. I use pink for freshman, yellow for sophomores, and blue for juniors. Seniors need to read all of them because they mostly pertain to them. This also makes it easier for underclassmen to glance through and find the few that are available for them.

After grade level, I put down the most basic requirements for each scholarship. Some may be as simple as "For seniors who will be attending college in the fall," "Who will be majoring in education" (i.e. music, communications, or engineering), "For females only," "minority students only," "students with community service hours," and "leadership skills," etc. This makes it much easier for the students to glance at them and see if they are eligible. Sometimes, they have to go on to read the requirements also. This might include a minimum GPA, financial need, numbers of letters of recommendation, transcripts, and any essay information. Students can read this bulletin and decide if they're eligible for this scholarship without having to read the entire application.

Then I type the amount and the number of scholarships offered, with the deadline last. If I don't see the words "postmark" with regards to the deadline as I stated previously, then I will assume that the deadline is when they want to receive the application. It's always better to be early than late. I mail the hardcopy applications one week early if the students give them to me by my deadline. You can't send the application in too early (unless the application has a start date).

I also type up a deadline list for all scholarships in order. This helps students get them organized. They either write down the scholarship titles and deadlines or simply take a picture on their phone. I try to go over the list with them because they always seem to miss something vital. I also date each bulletin, so if the student comes in on a regular basis, they don't have to reread each bulletin.

I try to always have the applications on hand whenever a student needs one. If I ever need more, I can find the master and request more copies. I strongly urge students to visit my 'scholarship wall' once a week so that they do not become overwhelmed by the amount of applications that I have.

I also have a book where students enter their name, major, and the college they plan to attend, so when I receive specific scholarships, I can find them and give them the application. I keep an updated GPA list as well, so if a general scholarship is GPA-based, I can then notify any students who are eligible.

I'm always available to answer questions for any confused student or parent as well and mention scholarships in class. Each year as they get older, I go more in-depth about information they need to know. My phone number is actually given out to anyone who needs it because I don't want anyone to lose out on a scholarship opportunity just because they were confused about the process. I had to set a time frame for calls to be received (not past 10 p.m.), and believe it or not, they always abide by it.

My job ranges from helping students search for careers or colleges, assisting in college applications, sponsoring a club, coordinating graduation, to attending an array of committees. But assisting students with scholarships is by far my favorite task and one of the most rewarding parts of my life.

I hope this books helps you (the student), your parents, and other school personnel understand scholarships, how to find them, and the best way to apply for them. Hopefully, you'll learn more than just a few words of wisdom from this book. I ardently hope you receive money to help with college costs and onward to fulfill your dreams.

An Overall Review:

- Keep your grades up—do not give up on them.
- Join organizations that interest you to encourage your involvment.
- Earn community service hours. This opens up more scholarship opportunities and helps others in need.
- Have your résumé ready
- Have your letters of recommenda- tion ready
- Read ALL directions.
- Write essays from your heart.
- Have someone proofread your work.
- Look for and apply for all eligible applications.
- Be neat and complete the entire application.
- Be on time. Don't miss deadlines.
- Apply, apply and apply again!
- Do not give up! You *can* do it!!

Appendix:
STATE AID RESOURCES

ALABAMA

Alabama Commission on Higher Education
100 North Union Street, Suite 205
Montgomery, AL 36104-3758
P.O. Box 302000
Montgomery, AL 36130-2010
Phone: (334) 242-1998
Toll-Free: (800) 960-7773 (AL Residents Only)

Alabama Department of Education
Gordon Persons Office Building
50 North Ripley Street
P.O. Box 302101
Montgomery, AL 36104-3833
Phone: (334) 242-9700

ALASKA

Alaska Commission on Post Secondary Education
Street Address:
3030 Vintage Boulevard
Juneau, AK 99801-7109
Mailing Address:
P.O. Box 110505
Juneau, AK 99811-0505
Phone: (907) 465-2962
Toll-Free: (800) 441-2962

Alaska Department of Education and Early Development
801 West 10th Street, Suite 200
P.O. Box 110500
Juneau, AK 99811-0500
Phone: (907) 465-2800
TTY: (907) 465-2815

ARIZONA

Arizona Commission for Postsecondary Education
2020 North Central Avenue, Suite 650
Phoenix, AZ 85004-4503
Phone: (602) 258-2435

Arizona Department of Education
1535 West Jefferson Street
Phoenix, AZ 85007
Phone: (602) 542-4361
Toll-Free: (800) 352-4558

ARKANSAS

Arkansas Department of Higher Education
423 Main Street, Suite 400
Little Rock, AR 72201
Phone: (501) 371-2000

Arkansas Department of Education
Room 304A
Four State Capitol Mall
Little Rock, AR 72201-1071
Phone: (501) 682-4475

CALIFORNIA

California Student Aid Commission
Street Address:
11040 White Rock Road
Rancho Cordova, CA 95670
Mailing Address:
P.O. Box 419026
Rancho Cordova, CA 95741-9026
Phone: (916) 526-7590
Toll-Free: (888) 224-7268

California Department of Education
1430 N Street
Sacramento, CA 95814-5901
Phone: (916) 319-0800

COLORADO

Colorado Commission on Higher Education
1560 Broadway, Suite 1600
Denver, CO 80202
Phone: (303) 866-2723

Colorado Department of Education
201 East Colfax Avenue
Denver, CO 80203-1704
Phone: (303) 866-6600

CONNECTICUT

Connecticut Department of Higher Education
Street Address:
61 Woodland Street
Hartford, CT 06105-2326
Mailing Address:
P.O. Box 150471
Hartford, CT 06106-0471
Phone: (860) 947-1800
Toll-Free: (800) 842-0229

Connecticut State Department of Education
State Office Building
165 Capitol Avenue, Room 312
Hartford, CT 06106-1630
Phone: (860) 713-6543
Toll-Free: (800) 465-4014

DELAWARE

Delaware Higher Education Commission
The Townsend Building
401 Federal Street, Suite 2
Dover, DE 19901
Phone: (302) 735-4120
Toll-Free: (800) 292-7935

Delaware Department of Education
401 Federal Street, Suite 2
Dover, DE 19901-3639
Phone: (302) 735-4000
Auxiliary Office:
John W. Collette Education Resource Center
35 Commerce Way
Dover, DE 19904

DISTRICT OF COLUMBIA

District of Columbia Public Schools
Division of Student Services
4501 Lee Street N.W.
Washington DC 20019
(202) 727-3688

Office of the State Superintendent of Education
State Board of Education
Suite 350N
441 Fourth Street NW
Washington, DC 20001
Phone: (202) 727-6436

FLORIDA

Office of Student Financial Assistance
State Department of Education
325 West Gaines Street, Suite 1314
Tallahassee, FL 32399
Phone: (850) 410-5180
Toll-Free: (888) 827-2004 (FL residents only)

Florida Department of Education
325 West Gaines Street
Tallahassee, FL 32399-0400
Phone: (850) 245-0505

GEORGIA

Georgia Student Finance Commission
State Loans and Grants Division
2082 East Exchange Place, Suite 245
Tucker, GA 30084
Phone: (770) 724-9000
Toll-Free: (800) 505-4732

Georgia Department of Education
2066 Twin Towers East
205 Jesse Hill Jr. Drive, SE
Atlanta, GA 30334-5001
Phone: (404) 656-2800
Toll-Free: (800) 311-3627 (Georgia residents only)

HAWAII

Hawaii State Postsecondary Education Commission
Office of the Board of Regents Room 209
2444 Dole Street, Room 209
Honolulu, HI 96822-2302
Phone: (808) 956-8213

Hawaii State Department of Education
Systems Accountability Office
1390 Miller Street, Room 411
Honolulu, HI 96813
Phone: (808) 586-3283

IDAHO

Idaho State Board of Education
Street Address:
Len B. Jordan Office Building
650 West State Street
Mailing address:
P.O. Box 83720
Boise, ID 83720-0027
Phone: (208) 332-6800
Toll-Free: (800) 432-4601 (Idaho residents only)

ILLINOIS

Illinois Student Assistance Commission
1755 Lake Cook Road
Deerfield, IL 60015-5209
Phone: (217) 782-6767
Toll-Free: (800) 899-4722

Illinois State Board of Education
100 North First Street
Springfield, IL 62777
Phone: (217) 782-4321
Toll-Free: (866) 262-6663 (Illinois residents only)
TTY: (217) 782-1900

INDIANA

State Student Assistance Commission of Indiana
402 West Washington Street
Indianapolis, IN 46204-2811
Phone: (317) 232-2350
Toll-Free: (888) 528-4719 (Indiana residents only)

Indiana Department of Education
State House
South Tower, Suite 600
115 W. Washington Street
Indianapolis, IN 46204-2795
Phone: (317) 232-6610

IOWA

Iowa College Student Aid Commission
603 E.12th Street, 5th Floor
Des Moines, IA 50319

Mailing Address:
Iowa College Aid
430 East Grand Avenue, FL 3
Des Moines, IA 50309-1920
Phone: (515) 725-3400
Toll-Free: (800) 383-4222 (Iowa residents only)

Iowa Department of Education
Grimes State Office Building
400 East 14th Street
Des Moines, IA 50319-0146
Phone: (515) 281-3436

KANSAS

Kansas Board of Regents
Curtis State Office Building Suite 520
1000 SW Jackson Street
Topeka, KS 66612-1368
Phone: (785) 296-3421

Kansas Department of Education
900 S.W. Jackson
Topeka, KS 66612-1182
Phone: (785) 296-3201
TTY: (785) 296-6338

KENTUCKY

Kentucky Higher Education Assistance Authority
P.O. Box 798
Frankfort, KY 40602-0798
Phone: (502) 696-7200
Toll-Free: (800) 928-8926

Kentucky Department of Education
Capital Plaza Tower
First Floor
500 Mero Street
Frankfort, KY 40601
Phone: (502) 564-3141

LOUISIANA

Louisiana Student Financial Assistance Commission
Office of Student Financial Assistance
Street Address
602 North Fifth Street
Baton Rouge, LA 70802
Mailing Address
P.O. Box 91202
Baton Rouge, LA 70821-9202
Phone: (225) 219-1012
Toll-Free: (800) 259-5626 x1012

Louisiana Department of Education
1201 North Third
P.O. Box 94064
Baton Rouge, LA 70804-9064
Phone: (225) 219-5172
Toll-Free: (877) 453-2721

MAINE

Finance Authority of Maine
Street Address:
5 Community Drive,
Augusta, ME 04332-0949
Mailing Address:
P.O. Box 949
Augusta, ME 04332-0949
Phone: (207) 623-3263
Toll-Free: (800) 228-3734

Maine Department of Education
Burton M. Cross State Office Building
23 State House Station
Augusta, ME 04333-0023
Phone: (207) 624-6600
TTY: (207) 624-6800

MARYLAND

Maryland Higher Education Commission
6 North Liberty Street
Baltimore, MD 21201
Phone: (410) 767-3300
Toll-Free: (800) 974-0203 (Maryland residents only)

Maryland State Department of Education
200 West Baltimore Street
Baltimore, MD 21201
Phone: (410) 767-0100
Toll-Free: (888) 246-0016

MASSACHUSETTS

Massachusetts Department of Higher Education
One Ashburton Place, Room 1401
Boston, MA 02108-1696
Phone: (617) 994-6950

Massachusetts Higher Education Information Center
700 Boylston Street
Boston, MA 02116
Phone: (617) 536-0200
Toll-Free: (877) 332-4348 (Massachusetts residents only)

Massachusetts Department of Elementary and Secondary Education
75 Pleasant Street
Malden, MA 02148-4906
Phone: (781) 338-3000
TTY: (800) 439-2370

MICHIGAN

Michigan Higher Education Assistance Authority
Office of Scholarships and Grants
P.O. Box 30462
Lansing, MI 48909-7962
(517) 373-3394
(888) 447-2687

Michigan Student Financial Services Bureau
P.O. Box 30047
Lansing, MI 48909-7547
Toll-Free: (800) 642-5626 x37054

Michigan Department of Education
Street Address:
608 West Allegan Street
Lansing, Michigan 48909
Mailing Address:
P.O. Box 30008
Lansing, MI 48909-7547
Phone: (517) 373-3324

MINNESOTA

Minnesota Higher Education Services Office
Minnesota Office of Higher Education
1450 Energy Park Drive, Suite 350
St. Paul, MN 55108-5227
Phone: (651) 642-0567
Toll-Free: (800) 657-3866

Minnesota Department of Education
1500 Highway 36 West
Roseville, MN 55113-4266
Phone: (651) 582-8200
TTY: (651) 582-8201

MISSISSIPPI

Mississippi Institutions of Higher Learning
3825 Ridgewood Road
Jackson, MS 39211-6453
Phone: (601) 432-6647
Toll-Free: (800) 327-2980 (Mississippi residents only)

Mississippi Department of Education
Street Address:
359 North West Street
Jackson, MS 39201
Mailing Address:
P.O. Box 771
Jackson, MS 39205-0771
Phone: (601) 359-3513

MISSOURI

Missouri Department of Higher Education
Street Address:
205 Jefferson Street
Jefferson City, MO 651101-2901
Mailing Address:
P.O. Box 1469
Jefferson City, MO 65102-1469
Phone: (573) 751-2361
Toll-Free: (800) 473-6757

Missouri Department of Elementary and Secondary Education
Street Address:
205 Jefferson Street
Jefferson City, MO 651101-2901
Mailing Address:
P.O. Box 480
Jefferson City, MO 65102-0480
Phone: (573) 751-4212
TTY: (800) 735-2966

MONTANA

Montana University System
Street Address:
2500 Broadway Street
Helena, MT 59601-4901
Mailing Address:
P.O. Box 203201
Helena, MT 59620-3201
Phone: (406) 444-6570

Montana Office of Public Instructions
Street Address:
State Capitol, Room 106
Mailing Address:
P.O. Box 202501
Helena, MT 59620-2501
Phone: (406) 444-2082
Toll-Free: (888) 231-9393 (Area code 406 only)

NEBRASKA

Coordinating Commission for Postsecondary Education
Street Address:
140 North Eighth Street, Suite 300
Lincoln, NE 68509
Mailing Address:
P.O. Box 95005
Lincoln, NE 68509-5005
Phone: (402) 471-2847

Nebraska Department of Education
Street Address:
301 Centennial Mall South
Lincoln, NE 68509
Mailing Address
P.O. Box 94987
Lincoln, NE 68509-4987
Phone: (402) 471-2295

NEVADA

Nevada Department of Education Northern Office
700 East Fifth Street
Carson City, NV 89701
Phone: (775) 687-9217

Nevada Department of Education Southern Office
9890 S. Maryland Parkway, Second Floor
Las Vegas, NV 89183
(702) 486-6458

NEW HAMPSHIRE

New Hampshire Postsecondary Education Commission
101 Pleasant Street
Concord, NH 03301-3860
Phone: (603) 271-3494

New Hampshire Department of Education
Hugh J. Gallen State Office Park
101 Pleasant Street
Concord, NH 03301-3860
Phone: (603) 271-3494
Toll-Free: (800) 339-9900
TTY: Relay New Hampshire 711

NEW JERSEY

Higher Education Student Assistance Authority
Street Address:
Four Quakerbridge Plaza
Trenton, NJ 08625
Mailing Address:
P.O. Box 540
Trenton, NJ 08625-0540
Phone: (609) 588-3136
Toll-Free: (800) 792-8670

New Jersey Department of Education
Street Address:
100 Riverview Plaza
Trenton, NJ 08625
Mailing Address:
P.O. Box 500
Trenton, NJ 08625-0500
Phone: (609) 292-4450
Toll-Free: 1-877-900-6960

NEW MEXICO

New Mexico Commission on Higher Education
New Mexico Higher Education Department
2048 Galisteo Street
Santa Fe, NM 87505-2100
Phone: (505) 476-8400
Toll-Free: (800) 279-9777

New Mexico Public Education Department
300 Don Gaspar
Santa Fe, NM 87501-2786
Phone: (505) 827-6330

NEW YORK

New York State Higher Education Services Corporation
99 Washington Avenue
Albany, NY 12255
Phone: (518) 473-1574
Toll-Free: (888) 697-4372

New York State Education Department
Education Building
89 Washington Avenue, Room 111
Albany, NY 12234
Phone: (518) 474-3852

NORTH CAROLINA

North Carolina State Education Assistance Authority
P.O. Box 14103
Research Triangle Park, NC 27709
Phone: (919) 549-8614
Toll-Free: (800) 700-1775 (North Carolina residents only)

North Carolina Department of Public Instruction
301 North Wilmington Street
Raleigh, NC 27601
Phone: (919) 807-3300

NORTH DAKOTA

North Dakota University System
State Student Financial Assistance Program
10th Floor, State Capitol
600 East Boulevard Avenue, Dept. 215
Bismarck, ND 58505-0230
Phone: (701) 328-2960

North Dakota Department of Public Instruction
Department 201
600 East Boulevard Avenue
Bismarck, ND 58505-0440
Phone: (701) 328-2260

OHIO

Ohio Board of Regents
30 East Broad Street, 36th floor
Columbus, OH 43215-3414
Phone: (614) 466-6000
Toll-Free: (888) 833-1133

Ohio Department of Education
25 South Front Street
Columbus, OH 43215-4183
Phone: (614) 995-1545
Toll-Free: (877) 644-6338
TTY: (888) 886-0181

OKLAHOMA

Oklahoma State Regents for Higher Education
655 Research Parkway, Suite 200
Oklahoma City, OK 73104
Phone: (405) 225-9100

Oklahoma State Department of Education
Oliver Hodge Building
2500 North Lincoln Boulevard
Oklahoma City, OK 73105-4599
Phone: (405) 521-3301
Toll-Free: (800) 247-0420

OREGON

Oregon Student Assistance Commission
Suite 100
1500 Valley River Drive
Eugene, OR 97401
Phone: (541) 687-7400
Toll-Free: (800) 452-8807

Oregon University System
P.O. Box 3175
Eugene, OR 97403-0175
Phone: (541) 346-5700
TTY: (541) 346-5741

Oregon Department of Education
255 Capitol Street, NE
Salem, OR 97310-0203
Phone: (503) 947-5600
TTY: (503) 378-2892

PENNSYLVANIA

Pennsylvania Higher Education Assistance Agency
1200 North Seventh Street
Harrisburg, PA 17102-1444
Phone: (717) 720-2509
Toll-Free: (800) 443-0646

Pennsylvania Department of Education
333 Market Street
Harrisburg, PA 17126-0333
Phone: (717) 787-7222
TTY: (717) 783-8445

RHODE ISLAND

Rhode Island Board of Governors for Higher Education &
Rhode Island Office of Higher Education
Shepard Building, Suite 524
80 Washington Street
Providence, RI 02903
(401) 456-6000

Rhode Island Higher Education Assistance Authority
560 Jefferson Boulevard, Suite 100
Warwick, RI 02886-1304
Phone: (401) 736-1100
Toll-Free: (800) 922-9855

Rhode Island Department of Elementary and Secondary Education
255 Westminster Street
Providence, RI 02903-3400
Phone: (401) 222-4600
TTY: (800) 745-5555

SOUTH CAROLINA

South Carolina Commission on Higher Education
1333 Main Street, Suite 200
Columbia, SC 29201
Phone: (803) 737-2260

South Carolina Department of Education
1006 Rutledge Building
1429 Senate Street
Columbia, SC 29201
Phone: (803) 734-8815

SOUTH DAKOTA

Department of Education and Cultural Affairs
South Dakota Board of Regents Suite 200
306 East Capitol Avenue
Pierre, SD 57501-2545
Phone: (605) 773-3455

South Dakota Board of Regents
306 East Capitol Avenue, Suite 200
Pierre, SD 57501
Phone: (605) 773-3455

South Dakota Department of Education
800 Governors Drive, #3
Pierre, SD 57501-2291
Phone: (605) 773-3134
TTY: (605) 773-6302

TENNESSEE

Tennessee Higher Education Commission
Parkway Towers Suite 1900
404 James Robertson Parkway
Nashville, TN 37243
Phone: (615) 741-3605

Tennessee State Department of Education
Andrew Johnson Tower, Sixth Floor
710 James Robertson Parkway
Nashville, TN 37243-0375
Phone: (615) 741-5158

TEXAS

Texas Higher Education Coordinating Board
1200 East Anderson Lane
Austin, TX 78752
Phone: (512) 427-6101
Toll-Free: (800) 242-3062

Texas Education Agency
William B. Travis Building
1701 North Congress Avenue
Austin, TX 78701-1494
Phone: (512) 463-9734
TTY: (512) 475-3540

UTAH

Utah State Board of Regents
Utah System of Higher Education
60 South 400 West
Salt Lake City, UT 84101-1284
Phone: (801) 321-7294
Toll-Free: (877) 336 — 7378

Utah State Office of Education
Street Address:
250 East 500 South
Salt Lake City, UT 84111-3204
Mailing Address:
P.O. Box 144200
Salt Lake City, UT 84114-4200
Phone: (801) 538-7500

VERMONT

Vermont Student Assistance Corporation
Street Address:
10 East Allen Street
Winooski, VT 05404
Mailing Address:
P.O. Box 2000
Winooski, VT 05404
Phone: (802) 655-9602
Toll-Free: (800) 642-3177
TTY: (800) 281-3341

Vermont Agency of Education
219 North Main Street, Suite 402
Barre, VT 05641
Phone: (802) 479-1030

VIRGINIA

State Council of Higher Education for Virginia
James Monroe Building
10th Floor, 101 North 14th Street
Richmond, VA 23219
Phone: (804) 225-2600

Virginia Department of Education
Street Address:
James Monroe Building
101 North 14th Street
Richmond, VA 23219
Mailing Address:
P.O. Box 2120
Richmond, VA 23218-2120
Phone: (804) 225-2420

WASHINGTON

Washington State Higher Education Coordinating Board
P.O. Box 43430
Olympia, WA 98504-3430
917 Lakeridge Way SW
Olympia, WA 98502
Phone: (360) 753-7800

State Department of Education
Office of Superintendent of Public Instruction
Street Address:
Old Capitol Building
600 South Washington Street SE
Olympia, WA 98501-1359
Mailing Address:
P.O. Box 47200
Olympia, WA 98504-7200
Phone: (360) 725-6000
TTY: (360) 664-3631

WEST VIRGINIA

West Virginia Higher Education Policy Commission
1018 Kanawha Boulevard, East, Suite 700
Charleston, WV 25301-2800
Phone: (304) 558-2101

West Virginia Department of Education
Building 5, Room 205
1900 Kanawha Boulevard East
Charleston, WV 25305-2440
Phone: (304) 558-2681

WISCONSIN

Wisconsin Higher Educational Aids Board Suite 902
131 West Wilson Street
Madison, WI 53703-3259
Phone: (608) 267-2206

Wisconsin Department of Public Instruction
Street Address:
125 South Webster Street
Madison, WI 53703-3474
Mailing Address:
P.O. Box 7841
Madison, WI 53707-7841
Phone: (608) 266-3390
Toll-Free: (800) 441-4563
TTY: (608) 267-2427

WYOMING

Wyoming Community College Commission
2020 Carey Avenue, Eighth Floor
Cheyenne, WY 82002
Phone: (307) 777-7763

Wyoming Department of Education
Hathaway Building, Second Floor
2300 Capitol Avenue
Cheyenne, WY 82002-0050
Phone: (307) 777-7690
TTY: (307) 777-8546

U.S. Department of Education
(Including SSIG Program
Student Financial Assistance Programs
Pell and State Grant Section)
400 Maryland Avenue, SW
Washington, D.C. 20202
Phone: (800)433-3243
TTY: (800) 730-8913

PUERTO RICO

Puerto Rico Council on Higher Education
P.O. Box 19900
San Juan, PR 00910-1900
(787) 724-7100

Department of Education
150 Calle Federico Costa
San Juan, PR, 00918
United States
(787) 759-2000

U.S. DEPARTMENT OF EDUCATION

Office of Postsecondary Education
U.S. Department Of Education
Office of Postsecondary Education
1990 K Street, N.W.
Washington, DC 20006
Phone: (202) 502-7750

Federal Student Aid
An Office of the U.S. Department of Education
400 Maryland Avenue, SW
Washington, D.C. 20202
Phone: (800)433-3243
TTY: (800) 730-8913

Index

35473899R00081

Made in the USA
Lexington, KY
04 April 2019